UNDERSTANDING THE ORACLE SERVER

Marina Krakovsky

For book and bookstore information

http://www.prenhall.com

Prentice Hall PTR
Upper Saddle River, New Jersey 07458

Library of Congress Cataloging-in-Publication Data

Krakovsky, Marina

Understanding the Oracle Server/Marina Krakovsky.

p. cm.

Includes Index.

ISBN 0-13-190265-2

1. Oracle (Computer file)   2. Relational databases.

3. Client/server computing.   I. Title.

QA76.9.D3K717   1995   95-25456

005.75'65--dc20   CIP

Editorial/Production Supervision: Lisa Iarkowski
Interior Design: Kerry Reardon
Acquisitions Editor: Mark Taub
Manufacturing Manager: Alexis R. Heydt
Cover Design Director: Jerry Votta
Cover Design: Design Source

 © 1996 Prentice Hall PTR
Prentice-Hall, Inc.
A Simon & Schuster Company
Upper Saddle River, NJ 07458

All product names mentioned herein are the trademarks of their respective owners.

The publisher offers discounts on this book when ordered in bulk quantities.
For more information, contact:

Corporate Sales Department
PTR Prentice Hall
One Lake Street
Upper Saddle River, NJ 07458
Phone: 800-382-3419
FAX: 201-236-7141
e-mail: corpsales@prenhall.com

Printed in the United States of America

10 9 8 7 6 5 4 3 2 1

ISBN 0-13-190265-2

Prentice-Hall International (UK) Limited, London
Prentice-Hall of Australia Pty. Limited, Sydney
Prentice-Hall of Canada, Inc., Toronto
Prentice-Hall Hispanoamericana S.A., Mexico
Prentice-Hall of India Private Limited, New Delhi
Prentice-Hall of Japan, Inc., Tokyo
Simon & Schuster Asia Pte. Ltd., Singapore
Editora Prentice-Hall do Brasil, Ltda., Rio de Janeiro

CONTENTS

PART II   ADMINISTRATION

PREFACE

The "you" in this book, whether the word is stated or implied, is the database administrator. Throughout, I assume that most of my readers are DBAs or other information-systems professionals who will work with the Oracle Server.

At the same time, this direct approach makes the book accessible and worthwhile to other readers, as well. If you are a programmer, you will learn enough about the Server to write applications that take advantage of the Server's features, instead of duplicating those features in your code. Furthermore, because the book is organized around broad database topics—such as security, integrity, and consistency—rather than by product features, you will quickly see how the Oracle Server solves the classic database problems. People who are new to Oracle products but have worked with other database systems, or students of database theory, will benefit the most from this organizational scheme. But even if your previous experience has taught you almost nothing about databases—perhaps you're a computer hobbyist, a freelance technical writer, or prospective Oracle employee—you will come away from this book with a good understanding of what the Oracle Server is all about. While product features and functions change with great frequency, relational-database fundamentals remain the same. By grounding descriptions of the product in a broader theoretical framework, I try to offer you lasting value, a quality which—just by the nature of the industry—few software manuals or after-market books have.

Nonetheless, this book is not for everyone. Even though it's written simply, it does assume you have a certain level of computer literacy. For example, you should understand such general terms and concepts as "operating system," "application," "memory," and "I/O." But, like me, you don't have to be a computer scientist to understand how the Oracle Server works.

The book is organized into two major sections. Part I (Chapters 1-4) introduces the subject and describes the architecture of the Server and of an Oracle database. Part II (starting with Chapter 5) describes classic database problems and major database administration tasks, and shows how the Oracle Server solves these problems.

Chapter 1 presents "the big picture," showing how the Oracle Server fits into the suite of Oracle products and into the client/server computing model.

Chapter 2 briefly explains the relational model and introduces its major components: the table, the column, and the row. It then describes the major features and commands of SQL, the language used to interact with the Oracle Server and to define and manipulate data in an Oracle database.

Chapter 3 describes how the Oracle Server organizes data. It describes various schema objects, tablespaces, the data dictionary, and other logical structures.

Chapter 4 discusses the physical file structure of an Oracle database, as well as the memory and process structures that the Oracle Server uses to manage data on behalf of users. It explains the importance of the SGA and the background processes, and explains how these structures work as part of the larger database management system.

Chapter 5 explains the major types of data integrity and shows how you can use the Oracle Server to create a database that conforms to various integrity rules. It describes the Oracle datatypes, integrity constraints, and programmatic methods of enforcing integrity rules.

Chapter 6 shows how the Oracle Server guarantees data consistency while allowing high concurrency. It describes the mechanics behind such features as row-level locking and multi-version read consistency.

Chapter 7 explains when to start up or shut down an Oracle instance and tells how to do so. It also describes some of the most important initialization parameters that you might set.

Chapter 8 gives guidelines for managing space usage, from the file level down to the block level. The aim is to strike a balance between high performance and efficient use of disk space.

Chapter 9 introduces the major ways to optimize performance. It discusses such topics as memory allocation and statistics-gathering, the query optimizer, and the use of indexes and hash clusters.

Chapter 10 describes the Oracle7 security features. It explains your options for identification and authentication, shows how to use privileges and roles, and introduces the Server's auditing features.

Chapter 11 explains how to protect your database against failure. It describes the types of failure, tells how to perform different types of backup, and explains how the Server performs recovery.

Chapter 12 describes the distributed processing capabilities of the Oracle Server. The chapter explains the creation and use of database links, the two-phase commit mechanism, and various replication options.

Chapter 13 introduces two major Oracle Server options which take advantage of multiprocessing computers. It explains the Parallel Server Option, which is designed for use on loosely coupled systems, and the Parallel Query Option, which can be used on any multiprocessing computer.

While *Understanding the Oracle Server* presents several advanced topics, it does so in ways that do not distract readers who only want to understand the basics. For example, many esoteric topics appear in sidebars, while the Server's advanced features and options are tucked away in the last two chapters. The main goal is to lay down a solid foundation for you to build on. If this book excites you about the capabilities of the Server and makes you comfortable enough with the subject to inspire you to explore further, my project will have been a success.

ACKNOWLEDGEMENTS

I'd like to thank the many people who helped me transform an idea into a polished product.

First, thank you to my editor at Prentice Hall, Mark Taub, who inspired me with this idea and kept me on track throughout this project. Without Mark's experience, guidance, and ability to break down a huge job into manageable chunks, this project might have been too daunting.

Thank you to Ken Glasser for introducing me to Mark.

Thank you to Bonnie Crater, Maria Pratt, Danny Sokolsky, Bronwyn Eisenberg, Jim Bisso, Ravi Shankar, and Dana Izenson for helping me find an incredible group of subject-area experts to review the manuscript.

And, of course, thank you to the reviewers themselves. My first technical reviewers, Joe Lumbley and Walter Schenk, suggested many areas for expansion. Special thanks to Joe for giving a non-Oracle perspective. I also feel privileged to have had each chapter reviewed by true subject-area experts, including Oracle programmers, performance engineers, and DBAs. These people, working under a tight deadline, gave generously of their expertise and time to ensure technical accuracy and clarity: Gita Gupta, Bob Jenkins, Jeff Cohen, Vipin Gokhale, David Sidwell, Thomas Albert, Sundar Viswanathan, Lynne Thieme, Woei-Chung Lee, John Nordlinger, Liff Stengaard Thomas, Bill Maimone, and Bill Waddington.

Sometimes, the best reviewer knows almost nothing about the subject before the review: Ephrem Wu, by looking at my work through the eyes of my model reader, was able to read for comprehensibility, asking the right questions and thus identifying information gaps to be filled. Thank you, Ephrem, for your tremendous help!

Thanks also go to my other friends and colleagues for their practical help and moral support: Cyndi Chin-Lee, Julie Gibbs, Thomas Albert, Brad Hochberg, Blake Sullivan, Catherine Skrbina, John Nordlinger, Linda Blatt, Christine Browning, and Jonathan Price.

In addition, I'd like to thank my former managers, Bonnie Crater and Tom Leah-Martin, for encouraging me in this endeavor and for giving me opportunities to learn about the Server as part of my job at Oracle. Thanks also to Beatriz Infante, Bob Pariseau, David Puglia, and David Schellhase in their official support. I also appreciate the use of Oracle's extensive documentation library. Oracle's manuals and course materials were a rich source of information for this book.

Several people who entered this project at a later stage deserve special praise. My copyeditor, Joanne Eglash, performed a thorough, substantive edit on a fairly technical and perhaps unfamiliar topic. Vantage Art turned my amateurish sketches into clear, professional illustrations. My production editor, Lisa Iarkowski, expertly brought all the pieces together into a polished product.

I'd also like to thank Marcy Levine and Dori Steinhauff, the editorial assistants on this project, for doing much behind-the-scenes work for this book.

Finally, a huge thank you to my parents, Rina and Gennady Krakovsky. I appreciate your help through every stage of this process, and especially during the summer: you gave me a quiet, carefree place to work when I needed it most.

THE BIG PICTURE

CHAPTER OVERVIEW

Oracle7, or Version 7 of the Oracle Server, is the world's leading database server. This chapter describes what a database server is and explains how the Oracle Server fits into the set of products produced by Oracle Corporation.

ORACLE7 AND CLIENT/SERVER

The leading database server in the world, with a larger installed base than any of its competitors, the Oracle7 Server is the flagship product of Oracle Corporation. Oracle produces hundreds of software products—from applications to application-development tools to office-automation products—and they all depend on the functions performed by the Oracle Server.

FRONT ENDS AND BACK ENDS

As in any client/server system, the database server in an Oracle configuration is the *back end*, doing central work that clients, or *front ends*, need. As you will see in later chapters, the Server has several complex responsibilities. It is inefficient for each application to try to handle all these responsibilities; one dedicated server can do the job.

Your company or department, for example, might have a system administrator with years of training and experience to help solve computer problems. While this specialist solves your system problems, you can focus on the work that you are good at—whether it be writing, programming, or marketing.

In the same way, the client/server model enables the server to focus on the complex tasks of database management, so that client applications can focus on their own responsibilities, such as presenting a usable interface. The people who design and write applications, then, don't have to be experts in database management because experts in that field have done that work in designing the server.

In addition, by keeping client tasks separate from server tasks, an information-systems professional can take maximum advantage of the strengths and weaknesses of various computers in the enterprise. For example, he or she can use several inexpensive desktop computers for running applications while using a single mainframe or minicomputer as the server platform. The large computer provides power and performance for server tasks, while the smaller computer presents a familiar, easy-to-use interface to an application user (see Figure 1.1).

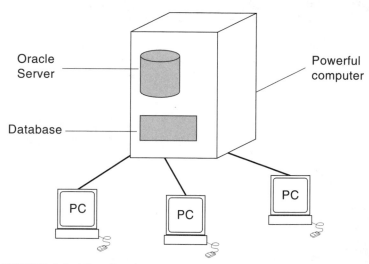

FIGURE 1.1 The client/server model divides the work among powerful, expensive computers and smaller ones that have more user-friendly interfaces.

The client/server model uses the economic principle of *comparative advantage*, using each hardware and software component to do what it's best at. It would be wasteful for a lawyer to spend her time filing papers and making photocopies, even if she can do so faster than her assistant. Because her true value lies in her analytic thinking and knowledge of the law, it's smarter for her to hire an assistant and use the extra time plying her trade. Similarly, it makes sense to divide the database work among an expensive, powerful machine and one or more cheaper computers.

THE MULTIPLE SERVERS OF ORACLE

Oracle Corporation now has several products in which a Server performs data-management tasks for multiple applications.

Media and Text Servers

You may have heard of the Oracle Media Server, the product designed to serve streams of video and sound to many users. This Server provides video "on demand" because it manages the storage and retrieval of many different movies and because each user can start and stop watching a movie at any time. To provide this simultaneous access at a high rate, the Oracle Media Server runs on massively parallel computers, such as the nCube, or on other computers with multiple CPUs.

A similar product, called Text Server, is designed specifically to manage large documents of unstructured text.

Oracle7 Workgroup Server

In addition, there are more lightweight variations on the basic Oracle7 Server. The Oracle7 Workgroup Server provides most of the features of the Oracle7 Server, but focuses on the needs of workgroups rather than entire enterprises. Thus, the Oracle7 Workgroup Server runs on a smaller set of operating systems—currently Windows NT, OS/2, NetWare, and several flavors of UNIX—and offers database administrators (DBAs) fewer choices for how to configure and tune their database systems. The advantage is that it comes pre-tuned to work efficiently in the workgroup environment and ships with graphical administration tools that are easy to learn and use. The Oracle7 Workgroup Server is also less expensive than the standard Oracle7 Server.

Personal Oracle7

Another low-end version of the Oracle7 Server is Personal Oracle7. This product, which runs on low-end operating systems such as Windows and OS/2, is designed for a single user, such as an application developer who wants to proto-type products on a local database. Like the Workgroup Server, Personal Oracle7 comes with database tools that are intuitive enough to be used by someone with little database administration background.

Oracle7 Server: The Focus of this Book

This book does not discuss the server products discussed above. Instead, it focuses on the core product—the Oracle7 Server—on which these other products are based. After reading this book, you will understand how the Oracle7 Server works, and this understanding will be a solid foundation for learning about the other products.

Unlike the other database servers, the Oracle7 Server runs on every popular computer platform, from personal computers to minicomputers and mainframes. Furthermore, it is a cooperative server, in that it can manage data stored on multiple computers. Because the statements users issue to query or modify data stored on several computers are the same as statements for accessing data stored on just one computer, users do not need to be aware of the underlying complexity. Similarly, applications developed for use with multiple computers and databases consist of the same code as applications developed for use on a single machine. Therefore, applications written for the Oracle7 Server are portable.

APPLICATIONS

Applications are programs that automate common business tasks. A word-processing application, for example, automates such processes as cutting and pasting, spell-checking, and formatting. Instead of writing a document in longhand or using a typewriter, then sending it to a typesetter for formatting, you can use your word processor to write, revise, proofread, and format your text.

Oracle applications—and other client/server applications—also automate business tasks. For example, a purchasing application automates such tasks as adding up the costs of items purchased, checking that a requestor has spending authority for the purchase amount, retrieving vendor information, generating a unique purchase order number, and so on. The Oracle Server has traditionally been used to manage corporate data: financial records; data about employees, customers, and vendors; and other textual or numerical data that is easy to organize in tabular form. Not surprisingly, then, most Oracle applications are designed with this type of data in mind. All such applications—whether designed to facilitate order entry, payroll, inventory management, revenue accounting, or capacity planning—are easy-to-use front ends to simplify the manipulation of corporate data.

EASE OF USE

Typically, these applications are fairly intuitive and easy to use. For example, most applications have screen interfaces that resemble traditional business forms. Thus, employees who are used to working with purchasing requisitions and purchase orders see familiar forms when they use financial applications. Furthermore, an electronic form is easier to fill out than its paper equivalent because it is a computer program with features to aid users. For example, most applications don't require users to type in a lot of information. Instead, the user typically gets a pop-up list of items, such as a list of approved vendors of a particular product. Then, using a mouse or cursor keys, the application user selects a choice from the list.

Because they are user-friendly, such applications improve productivity.

REDUCTION OF REDUNDANCY

Most common retail applications don't use the client/server model. That is, even while they automate certain tasks, they do not work in concert with each other or with a server and therefore do not achieve the level of efficiency that Oracle applications help achieve.

Because Oracle applications are designed as the front end for the Server, which performs the back-end work, companies can manage their information with great efficiency. Consider a standard business scenario. A customer fills out an order form. Then, a customer-service representative types up the order, perhaps into a computer. Later, a worker in order fulfillment uses the information to generate a pick slip so that other warehouse workers can fill the order. Once the order is ready, another person types up a packing list, while an employee in accounts payable adds up the prices and generates an invoice. Meanwhile, someone in inventory control must make note of the transaction to keep track of inventory levels of each part.

In this system, several people enter and re-enter essentially the same information so that each can use it for a different purpose. While the purpose and format vary, the basic information consists of parts, quantity, and cost. Repeating the steps with slight modifications, then, is a set of redundant efforts.

Client/server applications reduce or even eliminate this redundancy. Once the information gets entered, the Server and the database take care of the information content. As described below, the information only needs to be entered once—the applications do the rest, automating the labor of each of the people in the traditional scenario.

In the client/server scenario, the customer-service representative uses an order-entry application with an interface resembling a customer order form. Like any order form, this application has fields for customer name, address, items ordered, cost, and so on. The service representative enters this information, storing it in the database and thus making it available for use by other departments. Therefore, order fulfillment can use its own application to print out a pick slip with the necessary information formatted in the most useful way. In this case, the pick slip might show not only the parts and quantities ordered, but also the locator codes corresponding to the warehouse location of each part ordered. To obtain this information, the application would draw on data stored in the inventory database.

Once the order is ready, the picker simply presses a key to generate a packing list, a mailing label, and an invoice. Again, these materials get generated from information that already resides in the database from the initial entries by the customer-service representative. At the same time, the parts ordered get debited from the inventory database. If, as a result of this transaction, some parts fall below their re-order point, the application sends an electronic alert to the buyer, suggesting that the buyer replenish the stock of this part.

Each application, then, enables the different uses of this information, but the information only needs to be entered once (see Figure 1.2). Similarly, if a change needs to be made, one person makes that update, and the change is made throughout the relevant forms. For example, if a customer calls to increase the order quantity of a part, the customer-service representative makes the change in the order-entry application and starts the chain of events resulting in an efficiently filled, properly billed, and correctly accounted-for order.

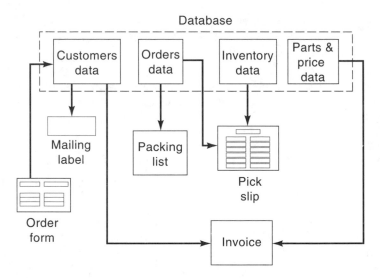

FIGURE 1.2 Storing all related information in a centralized database reduces redundant work by different departments. But while the data is centrally stored and managed, the applications that display the data meet the varied needs of each department.

ENFORCEMENT OF BUSINESS RULES

As you continue, you will see that the Oracle Server itself has ways of enforcing business rules, as well as more general rules to ensure the accuracy and integrity of stored data. In addition, however, Oracle applications can enforce other types of rules.

Many companies want to enforce certain cash-flow rules. For example, they want to make sure that a vendor does not receive payment until the company has received all purchases charged against a purchase order. In a centralized purchasing system—one in which the purchasing agent, the recipient of the goods, and the person in accounts payable are frequently not the same person—enforcing this business rule without software automation might be quite cumbersome and time-consuming. With Oracle applications, however, this rule is easy to enforce. The application does not allow the payment of an invoice until the recipient of the goods has confirmed receipt.

Even when only one person is involved in a traditional business process, the application's ability to enforce rules saves time, reducing the need for highly-skilled workers to perform what can be reduced to simple tasks. With the aid of a powerful and easy-to-use application, a data-entry clerk can quickly perform the tasks that might otherwise take even an experienced accountant hours to do. A purchasing agent who once spent much of the day on such mechanical chores as creating purchase orders can, with the aid of a smart application, instead focus on such higher-level tasks as conducting requests for proposal (RFPs) and qualifying vendors, tasks which require human intelligence.

CUSTOM APPLICATIONS

Sometimes, prepackaged Oracle applications and their built-in business rules are not enough. Let's say your company wants to make sure that no manager earns more than twice as much as any of his employees. You might want your human-resources application to enforce this rule. By creating your own variation of an Oracle application, you can enforce such rules.

To help you create custom applications, Oracle produces a set of products called *application-development tools*. The next section describes these tools.

APPLICATION-DEVELOPMENT TOOLS AND RELATED PRODUCTS

The applications discussed above perform common business tasks, saving time and human labor. Nonetheless, the applications themselves take time and labor to develop. If you have ever written a simple program that accepts a series of numbers and reports their sum, you have some idea of how long it would take to develop a complex program—such as a sophisticated and user-friendly spread-sheet application. Dozens of people working for several years might write such a program. All those person-hours would cost a company a lot of money. Nonetheless, as discussed earlier, a "canned" or pre-packaged application doesn't solve every problem the company has. Therefore, some development of custom applications is necessary in any large business.

To save all this time and money in developing custom applications, many businesses make use of Oracle's application-development tools. These tools, which include Oracle Forms, Oracle Graphics, Oracle Reports, and several others, do for software developers what applications do for administrative workers. We have already seen how applications save time by reducing redundancy and automating certain business processes; similarly, application-development tools reduce the time needed to develop applications.

How can software automate something as creative and non-mechanical as the development of applications? There are several answers.

LETTING THE TOOL HANDLE THE MECHANICS

Not all the work involved in developing applications is strictly creative. True, the design process requires analytical skills and creativity. But many of the tasks performed by programmers are mechanical and repetitive in that they involve certain problems to which other software designers have already found solutions.

For example, it takes creativity and human knowledge to write and edit a newspaper article, but in pre-computer days it also required a developed sense of copy-fitting and the patience to retype and manually rearrange pieces of an article. Now, with the availability of desktop-publishing programs, journalists can focus on the creative aspects of their trade while letting the computer take care of many of the mechanics. Similarly, programmers can use application-development tools to help them perform relatively simple tasks quickly, so that they can focus on the more challenging and interesting parts of their jobs.

Furthermore, many of the problems that commonly arise already have solutions. Recognizing the importance of reusability in software engineering, most language compilers come with certain predefined or *built-in* functions, routines, and libraries. Similarly, but on a larger scale, Oracle's application-development tools provide reusable objects, including common mathematical functions (such as the arithmetic and trigonometric functions), common interface and layout objects (such as buttons, scroll bars, and pop-up lists), and frequently-used routines.

HELPING OUT WITH CREATIVE WORK

While it makes sense that tools can help with mechanical or repetitious work, even the creative aspects of application development can benefit from the aid of good tools. A prime example are the products for computer-aided software engineering (CASE). These tools help application developers structure the design of their programming projects before the programmers begin coding. With CASE tools, developers can quickly draw entity-relationship diagrams and see the best ways to model their data.

Another area of programming where tools are useful is in writing reusable data-manipulation procedures. Such procedures, called *triggers*, are discussed in a later chapter. In summary, these pieces of code can be written much more quickly using a high-level language designed for data manipulation—like PL/SQL—than a host language like COBOL or C. By making this highly specialized language available as part of the tool, the application-development tool makes it easier for a programmer to write code related specifically to modifying and accessing data in an Oracle database. Sure, you could use a general, all-purpose spreadsheet program to manage your personal or family budget, but wouldn't it be faster to use an application designed specifically for managing your money?

THE 2000 SERIES

As we approach the millennium, application-development tools—and, in fact, software packages of all types—are becoming increasingly popular. It seems appropriate, then, that all of Oracle's current application-development and end-user tools come in product bundles with names containing the word "2000."

Designer/2000

This package includes products to aid in the design of Oracle databases and applications. It consists of CASE tools for modeling data, storing design rules, and generating prototype applications.

Developer/2000

This package includes the latest tools for creating client/server applications and designing reports. (Figure 1.3) These tools include Oracle Forms, Oracle Reports, Oracle Graphics, and Oracle Procedure Builder.

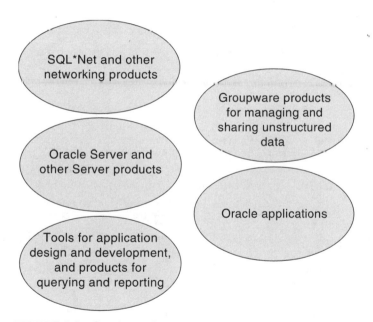

FIGURE 1.3 Oracle products.

Discoverer/2000

This package consists of two products: Oracle Browser and Oracle Data Query. Both are designed to make it easy for novice users—who are not familiar with the Oracle Server or SQL—to retrieve data from an Oracle database.

Groupware/2000

The tools in Groupware/2000 are designed for the needs of workgroups. Oracle Office includes features for scheduling meetings, coordinating room resources, and sending electronic mail. Oracle Book allows users to create hyper-text documents that can be shared, navigated, and annotated by users in a workgroup. Other products in the Groupware/2000 family also facilitate document management and sharing; all the Groupware/2000 products enable users to combine free-form information with the type of structured data that takes advantage of the power of a relational database managed by the Oracle Server.

Workgroup/2000

The Workgroup/2000 bundle includes Personal Oracle7, Oracle7 Workgroup Server, and products for wireless communication and rapid application development, including an object-based application development tool.

Workgroup/2000 gained attention as the first set of Oracle products to be distributed through the Internet. Oracle Corporation gave potential customers the opportunity to download Workgroup/2000 products from the World Wide Web for a free 90-day trial.

NETWORKING PRODUCTS

Whenever two or more products are installed on different machines, as they usually are in a client/server configuration, the only way for them to communicate with each other is through a network. The client and server machines must generally be connected physically through some type of cable. In addition, machines that wish to communicate with each other must be running compatible communications software, which governs the way data is to be transmitted. Oracle Corporation provides a product called SQL*Net, which forms part of the software component in this network model. SQL*Net and its protocol adapters make sure that Oracle data—SQL code and the results of queries—are properly transmitted and received. Each protocol and operating system has its own version of SQL*Net, so that applications can remain platform-independent and network-independent, and therefore portable.

Another Oracle product designed for the needs of moving data within a large network is the MultiProtocol Interchange, which translates packets of data sent via one protocol (such as TCP/IP) into a format that can be transmitted via another protocol (such as DECnet). Other Oracle products in the networking family manage the complexities of naming and addressing and make it possible for data to be sent in a secure, encrypted format.

PREVIEW OF CONCEPTS TO COME

Now that you have an understanding of how the Oracle products fit together, you are ready to begin your exploration of the Oracle Server. The next chapter discusses SQL, the high-level language used to interact with the Server.

Chapter 2

STRUCTURED QUERY LANGUAGE

CHAPTER OVERVIEW

SQL, or Structured Query Language, is the common name of the programming language used to define and manipulate data in a database. Several versions of SQL (pronounced at Oracle as "sequel") exist, but for the purposes of this book we do not deal with the distinctions. Instead, this chapter covers only the most common and most generic SQL commands. First, though, we briefly discuss the relational model, which describes the way data is logically organized in an Oracle database. Understanding the basics of the relational model helps to understand SQL and other concepts described later in this book.

THE RELATIONAL MODEL: COLUMNS, ROWS, AND TABLES

The main idea behind a relational database is that data is stored as a set of simple relations between tables or columns. A *column* represents a category of data, such as Store Name, while a *row* represents specific instances of those categories—for example, all the data for one store. The set of these rows and columns is a *table*. (Figure 2.1)

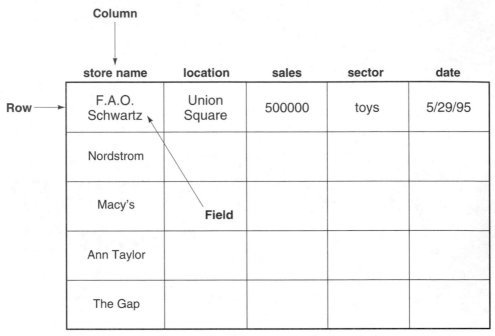

FIGURE 2.1   A table consists of rows and columns; the intersection of a row and column is a field.

The intersection of a row and column is called a *field*. The data inside a field is the value of that field. This concept is quite simple and is already familiar to you if you've worked with spreadsheets. However, the analogy between a database table and a spreadsheet ends there.

WHAT IS A DATABASE?

In its broadest sense, a database is a collection of related data. By this definition, any set of files dealing with the same topic is a database, even if the files are created on a word processor.

A good database, though, is more than just a collection of related data: it is a collection of data that is organized for quick access. One advantage of a relational database over a set of text files is that getting data out of it is much faster than getting data out of a flat-file database. You do not have to search through an entire database—or even an entire physical file—to find the data you need. Instead, you use a language like SQL to specify a condition; the database management system will return data that meets that condition.

Keep in mind that the relational model is only a logical, or conceptual, model. It does not govern how the data is physically stored. For example, data for two tables might be stored in one physical data file or spread across two or more data files. Similarly, several rows might be stored in one block on disk and one row can be stored in several blocks.

DEVICE INDEPENDENCE

With SQL, you don't have to worry about the precise location of the data in terms of physical devices. You only need to know which table contains the data, not how or where that table is stored. This feature makes SQL easier to program in than host languages: whereas a Pascal programmer must give the full file specification of all input files and output files used by the code, a SQL programmer merely needs to state the names of the tables and columns being manipulated. This extra level of abstraction—one degree more removed from the hardware than third-generation languages such as FORTRAN and C—is one reason SQL is called a fourth-generation language, or a 4GL.

If you want to retrieve a certain subset of data, you use SQL only to tell what you want to do; you don't need to explain how to do it. For example, suppose you want to fetch all rows in a table that have the letter X in the STATUS column. With another language, you might have to say:

❏ For every row in this table, look at column STATUS.

❏ Then, for every character in that field, see if the character equals X.

❏ If it does, print the values of all the fields in the row to standard output.

With SQL, in contrast, you issue one simple command that tells what sort of result you want. The Oracle Server then figures out what needs to be done to obtain that result. Because you don't use step-by-step procedures in SQL, it is a non-procedural language.

DATA DEFINITION AND DATA MANIPULATION

SQL commands fall into two types: data definition language (DDL) commands and data manipulation language (DML) commands.

Data definition includes all commands that relate to the set-up of the data. Commands for creating and altering databases, tables, and indexes, for example, are DDL commands.

Data manipulation, in contrast, lets you alter and fetch that data once it's defined; with DML commands, you can update the data, delete it, retrieve it, and so on.

The distinction between data definition and data manipulation resembles the distinction between structure and content. Data definition commands let you define the structure of the data, such as what tables you'll have with what columns, while data manipulation commands help you modify and access the contents of that structure.

SQL makes it easy to use both DDL and DML commands. In other languages, you must write a program that creates data structures by declaring variables. In the same program, you assign values to these variables. In SQL, on the other hand, issuing a typical DDL command creates a data structure that remains and is used by DML commands after the SQL script or command executes. By allowing the programmer to issue DDL commands independently from DML commands, SQL enables an easy client/server split: DBAs and programmers can use DDL commands to set up the data structures that can be used by many programs and individual DML commands.

Using SQL*Plus to Issue SQL Commands

To allow manipulation of the data in an Oracle database, Oracle Corporation ships a product called SQL*Plus. SQL*Plus is essentially a shell through which you enter SQL commands. You can issue commands one at a time or in batch mode, using SQL scripts that you run from SQL*Plus.

When you issue statements interactively—one at a time—you see a SQL prompt on the first line and numbered prompts on subsequent lines, until you enter a semicolon to indicate that the statement is complete. The examples in this book use these SQL*Plus conventions.

While you can also use SQL*Plus to format data into reports, it is much more efficient to use such powerful tools as Oracle Reports and Oracle Data Query.

COMMON COMMANDS

This section describes the most common SQL commands. These commands are not specific to Oracle's implementation of SQL. They exist in all versions of SQL because they handle such common data manipulation tasks as inserting, deleting, and retrieving data.

SELECT

The SELECT command is the most common SQL command because it is used to retrieve data from the database. Using the SELECT statement, you can retrieve any set of data from a table or set of tables.

A SELECT statement takes the following form:

```
SELECT <column or columns>
FROM <table or tables>
[optional clauses];
```

One frequently used optional clause is the WHERE clause, which is used to specify which rows to retrieve. The WHERE clause takes the following form:

```
WHERE <column> <condition> <value>
```

For example, to retrieve the names of all companies in your CLIENTS table that have bought more than $50,000 worth of merchandise from your company, you might issue the following SQL statement:

```
SQL> SELECT company_name, total_paid
  2   FROM clients
  3   WHERE total_paid > 50000;
```

The output of this query, or the *result set*, might look something like this:

```
COMPANY_NAME         TOTAL_PAID
----------------------------------
Simply Flowers       50500
Cakes by Charlie     53000
Allen's Autobody     78000
Lakewood Lamps       67000
```

A WHERE clause can specify more than one condition. For example, if you want to narrow down your search to only those clients who are located in the 94121 zip code, use the following SELECT statement:

```
SQL> SELECT company_name, total_paid
  2   FROM clients
  3   WHERE total_paid > 50000
  4   AND zip = 94121;
```

If only one of the clients who paid more than $50,000 is located in the 94121 zip code, then the result set would include only that client.

Notice that the rows in the result set of our first query are not in any particular order. To specify a sort order, you can use the ORDER BY clause. For example, to arrange the clients in alphabetical order, use the following command:

```
SQL> SELECT company_name, total_paid
  2   FROM clients
  3   WHERE total_paid > 50000
  4   ORDER BY company_name;
```

The output of this command would look like the following:

```
COMPANY_NAME          TOTAL_PAID
----------------------------
Allen's Autobody    78000
Cakes by Charlie    53000
Lakewood Lamps      67000
Simply Flowers      50500
```

The SELECT statement's ability to join tables to give a single result makes it extremely powerful. In designing a relational database, an application developer usually creates several tables to store different types of data, even if the data is somewhat related. For example, a university needs to store information about students, faculty, courses, and facilities. While some of this information is related—such as courses and the faculty that teach them—it gets stored in separate tables. The COURSES tables could contain such columns as course number, department, section code, and teacher code, while the FACULTY table could contain employee ID, employee name, job title, and salary. To retrieve related data from both tables simultaneously, use a SELECT statement in which you name both tables in the FROM clause and specify the join condition in the WHERE clause. A SELECT statement that selects data from multiple tables is called a *join*. (Figure 2.2)

```
SELECT section, last_name
FROM courses, faculty
WHERE dept = 'EE' AND num = 307
AND courses.teacher_id = faculty.emp_id;
```

dept	num	section	teacher_id	emp_id	last_name	first_name	salary
EE	307	A	10111	10111	Palmitieri		
EE	307	B	10267	10267	Abrams		
EE	315	A					
EE	315	B					
EE	356	A					
EE	400	A					
EE	400	B					
EE	420	A					
EE	450	A					
EE	460	A					
EE	460	B					

courses   **faculty**

FIGURE 2.2   A join selects related rows from two or more tables.

For example, suppose you want to find out who teaches the various sections of Electrical Engineering 307. The following query would give you the answer:

```
SQL> SELECT section, last_name
  2  FROM courses, faculty
  3  WHERE dept = 'EE' AND num = 307
  4  AND courses.teacher_id = faculty.emp_id;
```

The join condition in line 4 says that if a value of TEACHER_ID from the COURSES table matches a value of EMP_ID in the FACULTY table, then join the two rows into a single result. Even though SECTION is stored in one table and LAST_NAME is stored in another, the result set would look like the following, assuming there are only two sections of EE307:

```
SECTION      LAST_NAME
---------------------
A            Palmitieri
B            Abrams
```

INSERT

As its name suggests, this command is used to insert data into the database. Specifically, it is used to insert new rows into a table.

It uses the following syntax:

```
INSERT INTO <table>
VALUES <values>;
```

For example, to add a new row to the ORG table and fill in several pieces of information about Susan Expertlee, you might use the following command:

```
SQL> INSERT INTO org (emp_id, last_name, first_name, hire_date)
  2  VALUES (15590, 'Expertlee',   'Susan', '18-APR-95');
```

UPDATE

The UPDATE command also changes data in the database, but rather than inserting a new row, it simply changes the values within an existing row.

It uses the following syntax:

```
UPDATE <table>
SET <column> = <value>
[WHERE <column> <condition> <value>];
```

For example, to change the name of Expertlee's supervisor to Knowles, use the following command:

```
SQL> UPDATE org
  2  SET supervisor = 'Knowles'
  3  WHERE last_name = 'Expertlee';
```

To be syntactically correct, an UPDATE statement does not require a WHERE clause. If you leave out the WHERE clause, the Server applies the update to all the rows in the table. For example, if the previous example ended at line 2, then the statement would update all the rows, setting Knowles to be the supervisor for all employees in ORG.

DELETE

You can think of this command as the opposite of the INSERT command. Rather than adding new rows to a table, the DELETE command deletes rows that meet a stated condition. It uses the following syntax:

```
DELETE FROM <table>
[WHERE <column> <condition> <value>];
```

For example, to delete all rows from CUSTOMER in which the order number is less than 100, use the following command:

```
SQL> DELETE FROM customer
  2  WHERE order_number < 100;
```

As you might expect, the delete function is potentially dangerous. A good guideline is to try a SELECT first; if the SELECT returns the values you want to delete, then use the same condition in the DELETE command.

COMMIT

On the surface, the COMMIT command may seem trivial. Unlike other commands we've looked at, it takes no keywords or conditions. It simply tells the Server to save any work done in the current transaction—that is, any changes made since the last COMMIT or ROLLBACK command. Its syntax consists of one word:

```
COMMIT;
```

But don't brush it off because of its simplicity. As you will learn in later chapters, the COMMIT command is crucial to data concurrency and distributed processing.

ROLLBACK

The ROLLBACK command is, in a way, the opposite of COMMIT: it tells the Oracle Server to undo any work in the current transaction. While you have the option of rolling back work to a particular point, you can also simply issue the following command:

```
ROLLBACK;
```

This command will roll back any statements made after the last ROLLBACK or COMMIT, as if the statements had not been made.

FROM SQL TO PL/SQL

In your study of the Oracle Server and other Oracle products, you will come across references not only to SQL but also to PL/SQL. The PL stands for Procedural Language, denoting that PL/SQL contains procedural-language constructs that ordinary SQL lacks. The Oracle Server can split up certain DML operations and execute them in parallel, as discussed in Chapter 13. Still, the order of execution of SQL statements is predetermined and execution is non-iterative: select these rows; insert this row; delete that row. PL/SQL, in contrast, contains additional control structures, such as WHILE loops and IF-THEN-ELSE routines, that let the programmer control the flow of execution of SQL statements.

In addition to control flow, PL/SQL lets the programmer use variables and write error-handling additions to procedures. These features are particularly useful for writing code that underlies helpful, user-friendly applications. For example, suppose an application contains a block of code that gets a set of rows from one table and inserts those rows into another table. Now suppose a user clicks a button to execute that code using some criteria that he has entered, but no rows fit the criteria. What happens? Because no rows fit the condition, there is nothing to insert into the second table and an error occurs. If the block of code was written in ordinary SQL, the user would see that an error occurred. But unless the user knew much about the underlying tables and application code, he would not know why it occurred or how to fix it. If, however, the programmer had anticipated this situation and written the procedure in PL/SQL, then the procedure would give a meaningful error message, explaining what had happened and suggesting that the user re-enter the search criteria.

PL/SQL, then, is actually a superset of SQL. It adds to SQL's built-in logic an extra layer of control. With PL/SQL, a programmer can manipulate data in many ways; yet because it is a specialized database language, PL/SQL is simpler to use for database manipulation than a general-purpose language like Pascal or C.

LOGICAL STRUCTURES

CHAPTER OVERVIEW

In discussing the relational model in the previous chapter, we briefly described the logical structure of an Oracle database. The relational model—with its rows, columns, and tables—describes the basic underlying logic of an Oracle database. But as you can imagine, the full picture of how the Oracle Server organizes information is more complex. This chapter describes the other major logical structures that comprise an Oracle database.

SCHEMAS AND SCHEMA OBJECTS

Perhaps the best way to define schemas and schema objects is to give some examples. One example of a schema object is a table. As noted in the last chapter, a table is a set of rows and columns, as defined by the database administrator.

VIEWS

A *view* is a special way of looking at the data in a table or set of tables. As its name implies, a view is a glimpse at the data, a partial picture. Views do not them-

selves contain data; rather, they obtain data from their *base tables*. (Figure 3.1)
Thus, a view is a *virtual* object.

For example, let's say you have a table containing employee information that
is called EMPINFO. As a database administrator, you want to make some of this
information available to everybody at the company, so that employees can find out
the office locations of their co-workers. But, of course, you don't want to divulge
company-confidential information.

How do you allow all employees to view only some of the information? You
create a view based on EMPINFO. This view, EMPVIEW, contains only some of
the columns from EMPINFO. EMPINFO, then, is the base table for EMPVIEW.

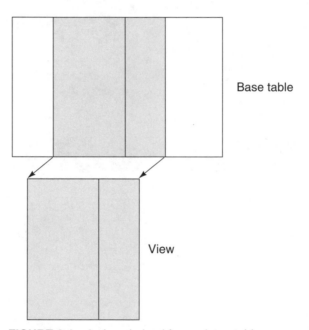

Base table

View

FIGURE 3.1   A view derived from a base table.

As you continue in this book, you will see other ways to implement security
measures—that is, to control who has access to what information. For now, just
keep in mind that a view is a schema object that DBAs use to restrict access to data.

Also, remember that a view is not just a window onto the base tables. In general, you can use a view for the same tasks as a table: you can query it, update it,
insert new data into it, and base another view on it. With some views, there are
exceptions to what you can do. For example, a view that is defined in terms of a
join between two or more tables cannot be modified—in other words, you cannot

insert, delete, or update data in the view. In general, though, you can think of a view as a virtual copy of data in one or more tables.

In fact, anything you do to a view affects the base table. Suppose you've given a set of users the right to update a view. If one of the users changes the address of an employee in ORGVIEW, the employee's address changes in the base table ORG, as well.

SEQUENCES

A *sequence* is another type of schema object. As its name might suggest, it is a sequential list of values for a special column in a table.

Any arithmetic series—ascending or descending—can be a sequence. In other words, a sequence can be a set of numbers separated by either positive or negative intervals. Each of the following is a sequence:

1	2	3	4	5	6	7
100	200	300	400	500	600	700
14	12	10	8	6	4	2

By definition, a sequence codes each new row of a table with a unique number. This can be useful for several reasons. First, it provides an easy way to query a particular row. For example, suppose Stanley, a purchasing agent, wants to find out the status of Susan Expertlee's current order. He might query by Susan's name, but the result of the query might be several orders, so Stanley would have to look through all of them for Susan's current order. But if a sequence exists for the table, then Stanley can simply query by purchase order number to find the exact order he wants.

Another benefit of having a sequence is easy sorting. By looking at two or more sequence numbers, you can easily tell the order in which the rows were created—assuming, of course, that you know whether the sequence is ascending or descending.

Perhaps the greatest benefit of using an automatically-generated sequence is to speed up transaction processing in a multi-user environment. Whenever a user inserts a new row, the Server automatically assigns it the next value in the sequence. If the Server does not perform this centralized role, each application has to ensure that users are not assigning duplicate numbers. Whenever several applications are inserting data into the same database, the Server is the only utility equipped to handle this problem.

Because it guarantees unique values, a sequence can serve as a table's *primary key*. We will discuss the concept of primary key in Chapter 5.

INDEXES

To help the Oracle Server retrieve data from your database more efficiently, you can create one or more *indexes* for the database. Without an index, the Server would have to scan the entire table to find the information you need. With the right index, the Server goes straight to the information.

A table that has an index is called an *indexed table*.

How does an index work? When you create an index on a particular column or set of columns, you are really telling the Server to note the physical address of the data block that corresponds to each row value. The physical address is analogous to a page number in a book's index: using the index, the Server goes directly to the physical address corresponding to the index entry, thus avoiding the extra disk I/O that would be necessary if the Server had to search every block. (Figure 3.2)

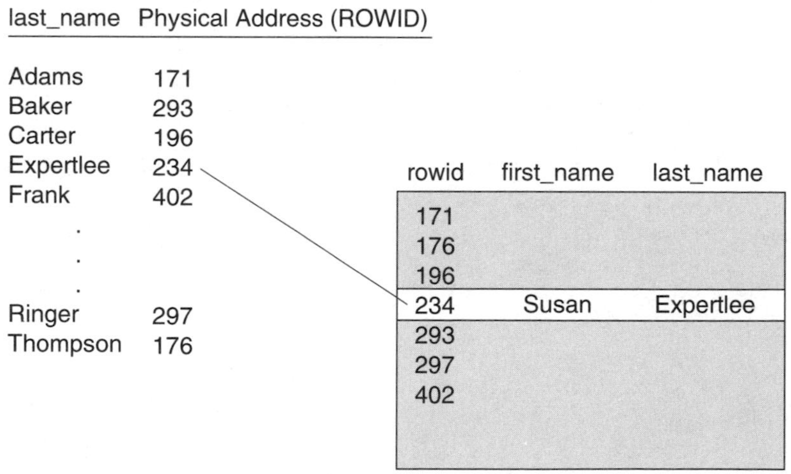

last_name   Physical Address (ROWID)

last_name	Physical Address		rowid	first_name	last_name
Adams	171				
Baker	293				
Carter	196				
Expertlee	234		171		
Frank	402		176		
.			196		
.			234	Susan	Expertlee
.			293		
Ringer	297		297		
Thompson	176		402		

FIGURE 3.2 An index speeds up queries.

The DBA and the application developers are the only users who really need to consider indexes. Ordinary users issue the same SQL statements regardless of whether an index exists. When the Server *parses* the statement, it decides whether to use an index (if, of course, one is available). Also, the Server automatically updates the index each time a user makes a relevant change to the database.

Parsing

To parse a statement means to break it down so it can be executed. Before parsing, a statement looks like a string of characters. When the Oracle Server parses a SQL statement, it first checks to make sure the statement contains no syntax errors. After validating the statement, the Server allocates a shared SQL area for its parsed representation, some-times called the *parse tree*. Once the parsed representation resides in a shared SQL area, it can be reused; that is, subsequent issues of the same statement—even if they come from different users or different applications—do not have to be parsed. As part of the parsing process, the Server chooses how best to execute the statement. In other words, it determines the execution plan.

But while the Server keeps the index up-to-date, the database users—including not only the DBA and the application developer, but also the end users—do have a role in making sure indexes are doing their job. After all, an index is only effective if users frequently query by the indexed column.

For example, suppose you have created an index on the ORDER_NUMBER column of a table used by the Purchasing department. If users query by purchase order number, the data for the corresponding purchase order should appear much more quickly than if no index existed. But suppose the Purchasing department starts getting calls from people who don't know the purchase order numbers: they only know what items they requisitioned and, in some cases, the name of the vendor. Purchasing agents will notice that performing these queries takes longer than performing queries by order number. Because of such delays, the application developer and the DBA should consider building another index on these frequently queried columns.

You might think that since each index speeds up data retrieval, the key to fast retrieval is to have many indexes. But a heavily indexed database has its drawbacks. Because the Server updates each index whenever a user manipulates the data in the underlying table, multiple indexes slow down some operations, specifically those that involve UPDATE and INSERT statements.

A good DBA and developer, therefore, must weigh the data-retrieval benefits of an index against the performance costs of data updates, and must create indexes only on those columns where the benefits outweigh the costs. A thorough analysis of the SQL statements most commonly used against a particular database will tell the DBA which indexes are most beneficial and cost-effective.

CLUSTERS

Another way of reducing data-retrieval time is to store data in *clusters*. A cluster consists of tables or rows in a table stored physically close to each other.

The most common use of clusters is to store data that is frequently accessed together. For example, a single table might store information about employees in different departments. However, each department would only need to generate reports about its employees. The most logical way to cluster the data on disk, then, is by department. The rows for all employees of a particular department would be concentrated in one disk block or in just a few contiguous blocks. The Oracle Server would not have to perform many reads to fetch that data.

The column or columns by which clusters are formed is called the *cluster key*. In the example above, DEPARTMENT is the cluster key. (Figure 3.3)

Another use of clusters is to store tables that are related—that is, tables that share a column. You can create a cluster having as its cluster key the name of the shared column. That way, the shared values are only stored once. If users frequently query the tables together, then only one I/O operation (instead of two) is necessary to perform the query.

For example, a university might need a COURSES table and a FACULTY table. To generate a report of all courses, including who teaches each course, the Server would need to read from both tables: while the COURSES table might give the employee number of the professor teaching the course, only the FACULTY table would list the professor's name. But if the tables were stored in a cluster in which EMP_NUMBER were the cluster key, then only one read would be necessary to fetch data from both tables. An added benefit of storing data this way is that it takes up less disk space: each cluster key value is stored only once.

As with indexes, the presence or absence of clusters is completely transparent to users (except, hopefully, for the performance gain).

emp_id	last_name	first_name	department	
			Manufacturing	
			Manufacturing	**Disk block**
			Manufacturing	
			Engineering	
			Engineering	**Disk block**
			Engineering	
			Marketing	
			Marketing	**Disk block**
			Marketing	

FIGURE 3.3   A table clustered by the DEPARTMENT cluster key. Each data block stores data for a single department.

DATABASE LINKS

A *database link* is the logical pathname of a remote database. While referring to a remote database, the database link actually belongs to the schema of the local database—that is, the database from which the link was created.

Once created, the database link allows a user of the local database to retrieve data from a remote database. For example, suppose you've created a database link called UK_INV.FLOWERS.COM from the schema of US_INV. Now, user SUSAN on database US_INV can query the table ORDERS by issuing the following command:

```
SQL> SELECT * FROM orders@uk_inv.flowers.com
```

We will discuss database links in more detail in the context of distributed processing in Chapter 12.

SYNONYMS

In languages like English, a synonym is a word that has the same meaning as another word. In Oracle terminology, a *synonym* is an alternative name for a schema object. For example, to make it easier for end users to refer to a database link with a lengthy name, you might create a short synonym for the database link name.

If you are a DBA, then, by using a synonym, you're not only making life easier for the end user, you're also making life easier for yourself. That is, if you move your database to another machine or even another city, you won't have to explain the change to your users; instead, you can simply redefine the synonym so that users can continue using the same name for what to them is the same object. (Figure 3.4)

PROCEDURES

As in most third-generation languages—including C and Pascal—a *procedure* or function is a set of commands designed to perform a specific task. In Oracle terminology, a procedure is a set of SQL or PL/SQL statements. To make a procedure reusable, you can store it in the database.

Why might you want to create a stored procedure? By storing a procedure in a database, you make it accessible to all applications that use the database. This has two benefits. First, it makes application development more efficient because each programmer only needs to make procedure calls instead of having to code each procedure. Second, it makes the application work faster because the statements comprising the procedure do not have to travel between the application and the database server, which might be on different machines in a network.

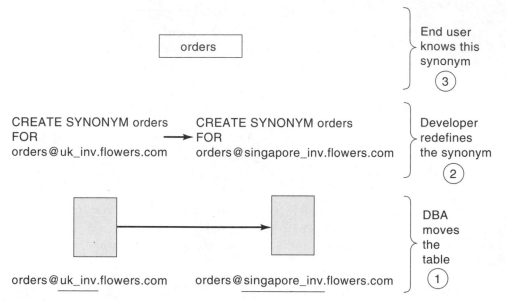

FIGURE 3.4 The end user is unaware that a table was moved so long as the developer or DBA redefines the synonym that the user was using.

PACKAGES

A package is another type of program unit that is considered an object in a user's schema. Larger than a procedure, a *package* is a set of related procedures and functions. In some cases, a package is really a full program, written completely in PL/SQL.

Now that you have a basic understanding of tables, views, synonyms, and so forth, you comprehend the concept of *schema objects*. The set of schema objects for a particular user is called the user's *schema*.

TABLESPACES

Earlier we said that a database consists of a set of tables. It is also true that a database consists of one or more *tablespaces*. Figure 3.5 illustrates the relationship between a database and its tables and tablespaces.

Like a table, a tablespace is a logical area of storage. A tablespace corresponds not only to one or more tables, but to one or more data files. Since a data file is a physical structure, we will discuss it in the next chapter.

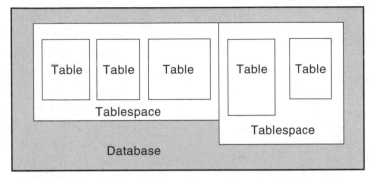

FIGURE 3.5   The relationship between a database and its tables and tablespaces.

Every Oracle database has at least one tablespace: SYSTEM. This tablespace holds the *data dictionary*. You can think of a data dictionary as a "meta-tablespace," because it holds tables which contain information about the database, as discussed later in this chapter.

SEGMENTS

A segment is a unit of logical storage. The Server allocates a segment for storing each kind of information needed by the database. The two most important types of segments are *data segments* and *rollback segments*. In addition, each table can contain an *index segment* and a *temporary segment.*

DATA SEGMENTS

A data segment stores the type of database information that we usually mean when we say "data." For example, in an employee table, the data segment stores such information as the names of the employees, their hire dates, and so forth. In an inventory table, the data segment stores part numbers and quantities on hand.

ROLLBACK SEGMENTS

A rollback segment stores information about database transactions. If for some reason a set of transactions needs to be *rolled back,* or canceled, the Server uses the data in the rollback segments to make accurate rollbacks. You will learn more about rollback segments in future chapters, when we discuss data concurrency and data recovery.

INDEX SEGMENTS

An index segment stores data for indexes created for a table.

TEMPORARY SEGMENTS

A temporary segment is a work area for executing certain SQL operations, such as some sorting operations, that cannot be performed in memory. These segments are temporary because they are deallocated after the operation requiring them completes.

EXTENTS

An extent is a unit smaller than a segment. That is, several *extents* make up a segment. (Figure 3.6)

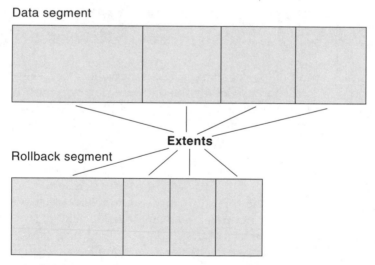

FIGURE 3.6 Several extents make up a segment.

Technically speaking, an extent is a set of contiguous data blocks used to store a particular type of information. Just as there are different segments for rollback data, index data, temporary data, and so on, there are different types of extents. Since a segment consists of extents, the Server allocates an additional extent to a segment whose space is full.

To allocate an additional extent, the Oracle Server searches through the tablespace containing the segment. In this tablespace, it tries to find a contiguous set of data blocks that are at least the size of the previous extent. Don't worry about the Server's actual algorithm for finding the chunk—just keep in mind that each new extent must use at least the same number of blocks as previous extents, and that these blocks must be contiguous.

DATA BLOCKS

A data block is the smallest logical unit of storage. Several data blocks comprise an extent (Figure 3.7), and one or more extents make up a segment. Though a data block is just a logical structure, it does correspond to some amount of physical disk space—that is, a certain number of bytes.

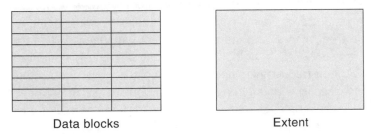

Data blocks   Extent

FIGURE 3.7   Several data blocks make up an extent.

Just how many bytes depends on two factors. First, the default number of bytes per data block depends on your operating system. Second, if you want to override the default, you can set another value in the initialization parameter DB_BLOCK_SIZE in your initialization parameter file, sometimes called the INIT.ORA file.

What exactly does a data block contain? As shown in Figure 3.8, each data block consists of the following:

❑ row data—the actual data contained in rows or parts of rows of a table

❑ free space—space that can be used for adding new rows

❑ block information—information about such items as block address, segment type, the table and row(s) that use the block, and other header information.

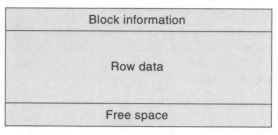

A single data block

FIGURE 3.8   The contents of a data block.

The Initialization Parameter File

The initialization parameter file, sometimes called the INIT.ORA file, is a text file that the Server reads on instance start-up. It tells the Server which initial values to use for various Server parameters. Some of the parameters are simple and contain information about the name of the database associated with the instance and the pathnames of various files. The values of other parameters—such as those that specify how many buffers to store in the SGA, how frequently to update checkpoints, what the maximum number of processes is—can have a great impact on system performance. There are no absolute optimal values for the initialization parameters: what is best in one scenario is not right for another. By wisely editing the INIT.ORA file, a sample copy of which comes with the Oracle Server software, the DBA can improve the performance of the Oracle Server at his or her particular site.

DATA DICTIONARY AND ITS VIEWS

The *data dictionary* of an Oracle database is a set of tables and views that contains information about that database.

What sort of information does the data dictionary contain? Along with information about the database's logical structures, the data dictionary holds information about the database's users—that is, their usernames and access privileges. Furthermore, it stores information about the *integrity constraints*, or rules, imposed upon the database. The data dictionary also keeps track of which users have queried the database or made updates. In other words, it contains data-definition information.

Like an ordinary dictionary, the data dictionary is a reference tool; therefore, you cannot modify it. And why would you want to? The Server automatically updates the data dictionary whenever you issue a data-definition command on the database to which the dictionary belongs. You will recall from Chapter 2 that data-definition commands (also called DDL commands, for Data Definition Language) are those SQL statements that alter the structure of the database. Therefore, if you add a new user, change a user privilege, or create a new table, the Server will change the data in the data dictionary.

How do you refer to the data dictionary? Because it is comprised of tables and views, you query it the same way you query a regular database—using SQL's SELECT statement. In most cases, you will be querying views—not tables—because unlike the base tables, the data dictionary views are in a format that is easy for a user to understand. For example, to see the names of all database links accessible to you from your database, you would enter the following command:

```
SQL> SELECT * FROM all_db_links;
```

Oracle's documentation explains the syntax for such a query and provides a complete list and description of all the data dictionary views.

From this discussion, you might get the idea that the Server updates the data dictionary, while users query it. In reality, the Server is also constantly querying the data dictionary. For example, each time a user performs an operation on the database, the Server checks the data dictionary to make sure that the user has the privilege to perform that operation. Therefore, the data dictionary is not only a useful reference tool for the DBA or user, but really an essential tool for the Server itself. Without a working data dictionary, you cannot use the database.

INSTANCES

An instance is one of the most important but most often confused terms in the Oracle lexicon. Many people use the term *database* when they really mean *instance*.

An Oracle instance is the combination of memory buffers and the background processes that manage transactions. This idea will become clearer in the next chapter. For now, keep in mind that an instance is not a database: whereas a database is a set of files, an instance is essentially a set of processes. In fact, in a parallel server configuration, several instances can share a single database.

PHYSICAL, MEMORY, AND PROCESS STRUCTURES

CHAPTER OVERVIEW

The information you learned in the last chapter gives you a good foundation for how an Oracle database is organized. This chapter completes your basic understanding of the architecture of an Oracle database by explaining the physical structures that correspond to the logical ones described in Chapter 3. It also explains the architecture of the Server itself by discussing the role of memory and of the processes that make up an instance of the Oracle Server.

ARCHITECTURE SUMMARY

All the parts are interrelated: any explanation of one part requires at least a basic understanding of the others. Therefore, this section summarizes the basic concepts, followed by more detail in subsequent sections.

A database consists of several files. Some of these files, the data files, store the main data of the database. Other files, the redo log files, store entries for all transactions made to the database; these are necessary in order to recreate data files correctly in case of a system failure. One file, the control file, stores information about the other files.

Constantly reading data from files on disk, however, is time-consuming. Therefore, the Oracle Server caches frequently-used data in memory, in an area called the SGA, or System Global Area.

To move data between the SGA and the files, and to perform other necessary operations, the Oracle Server uses many different processes.

SYSTEM GLOBAL AREA (SGA)

The System Global Area (SGA) is one of the most important concepts about the Oracle Server. To say that it is an area of computer memory used to hold information for a particular instance—which it is—does not do the SGA justice.

PURPOSE OF THE SGA

To really understand the importance of the SGA, you must understand the high cost of disk I/O. Disk I/O, which occurs when a computer writes data to disk or reads data from disk, is a time-consuming operation. It takes thousands of times longer to read data from a disk than it does to fetch it from memory. This ratio may not seem significant when comparing one read from disk with one read from memory, where the difference may be seconds versus nanoseconds. But the performance difference becomes extremely noticeable when you calculate the time it takes to perform real-world tasks such as generating reports that require thousands of reads.

The idea behind the SGA, then, is to allow users to read data from memory instead of disk. Thus, rather than write to disk and read from it, database users can share the information that gets accumulated in the SGA.

To understand the SGA, let's take a look at its parts. (Figure 4.1)

DATABASE BUFFER CACHE

This part of the SGA stores *database buffers*; in other words, it contains recently-used data blocks. Since chances are that recently-used data is data that is used frequently, keeping data in the buffer cache helps to reduce reads from disk. To learn more about how this works, see the section called "How the Server Uses the Database Buffer Cache."

REDO LOG BUFFER

While the database buffer cache stores data that will ultimately go into data files, the *redo log buffer* stores data that will go into the redo log files, which list all the changes of all transactions against the database.

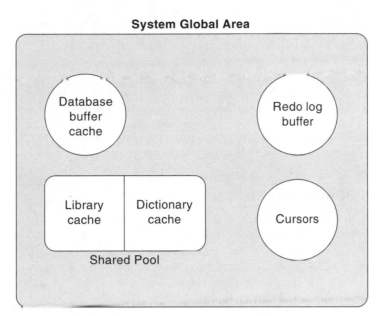

FIGURE 4.1 Contents of the SGA.

SHARED POOL

The *shared pool* consists of two caches: the library cache and the dictionary cache.

Library Cache

The *library cache* mainly contains PL/SQL packages and other SQL units, along with the information necessary for processing them efficiently.

Dictionary Cache

The *dictionary cache* is that part of the shared pool which contains the most frequently asked questions about the data dictionary. Generally, the most frequently asked questions are queries issued by the Server itself, such as queries to validate access privileges.

CURSORS

Information about shared *cursors*—which are either explicitly or automatically declared pointers corresponding to particular SQL statements—is also cached in the SGA. The cursor cache keeps information that will enable the Server to re-execute a SQL statement that has previously been executed, without starting over. This information includes the statement's *parse tree* (the parsed representation of a SQL statement) and the *execution plan* (the algorithm for executing the statement). As a result of caching this information, the Server can process repetitions of the same SQL statement more quickly than it did the first time the statement was issued.

Sometimes people refer to the SGA as the "Shared Global Area," because several users share the data in the SGA.

PROCESSES

The Oracle Server and its client programs use many processes to do their work. We can group them into user processes, server processes, and background processes.

USER PROCESSES

When you start a program that depends on the Oracle Server, a *user process* starts. These client programs include programs written using Oracle's application-development tools, programs written using other companies' application-development tools, or programs written in standard programming languages. Regardless of how such programs are written, they have one element in common: they query or update an Oracle database.

Since such client programs are not part of the Oracle Server, user processes are not Oracle Server processes. In fact, they can begin startup even if the Oracle Server is not running, though they won't get far: before a user can manipulate a database, the Oracle Server must be running.

SERVER PROCESSES

If an instance of the Oracle Server is running, one or more *server processes* are running. Whether more than one server process is running depends on the value of the initialization parameter SINGLE_PROCESS. If set to TRUE, then the instance runs with only one server process. Otherwise, the instance has multiple processes and can thus serve more than one user.

The server processes, then, handle the requests of the user processes. When a user issues a query, for example, a server process finds the query result. If more users are issuing queries and making other demands on the Oracle Server, then more server processes are necessary to handle these requests. Determining how many server processes to keep running is the job of one of the background processes.

BACKGROUND PROCESSES

The *background processes* help the server processes by performing specialized tasks.

DBWR: Database Writer

This is perhaps the most important of the background processes because it is responsible for writing modified data from buffers in the database buffer cache to data files on disk. (Figure 4.2)

Single-Task versus Two-Task Configuration

On some operating systems, notably MVS and OpenVMS, the work of both the user process and the server process can be handled by one process. This configuration, called *single-task*, is efficient because one process obviously requires less system overhead than two. For this configuration to work, though, both the Oracle Server and the client application must be running on the same machine. By running a database system in single-task mode, you give up the benefits of a client/server system.

The two-task configuration, the alternative to single-task, is the configuration discussed throughout this book.

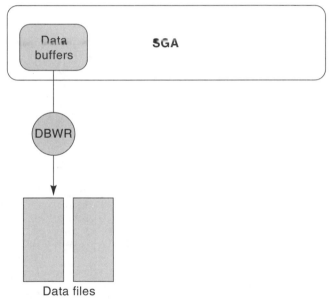

Data files

FIGURE 4.2 The DBWR writes data from data buffers to data files.

To achieve good performance, DBWR performs *deferred writes*. This means that it does not write to disk as soon as a user commits a transaction; instead, it waits until an event occurs that indicates it is a good time to write. There are several such events:

❑ A checkpoint occurs. A checkpoint always occurs when a redo log file fills up, but can occur on other occasions, as determined by the DBA.

❑ The dirty list, which contains modified buffers, becomes full.

❑ A server process does not find a free buffer after searching a predefined number of buffers in the LRU list; a DBA sets this number using the DB_BLOCK_MAX_SCAN_CNT initialization parameter.

❑ A time-out occurs (if DBWR has been inactive for three seconds).

LGWR: Log Writer

The LGWR process does for redo logs what DBWR does for buffered data blocks: it writes them to disk. Specifically, LGWR moves data from the SGA's redo log buffer to the redo log files on disk. (Figure 4.3)

Why does LGWR do this? Recall that DBWR performs deferred writes, thus leaving a short period in which modified data in the database buffer cache is not saved to data files on disk. To ensure that this data does not get lost in case the instance dies, it must be stored on disk elsewhere. That task—saving changes to a redo log file—is the job of LGWR.

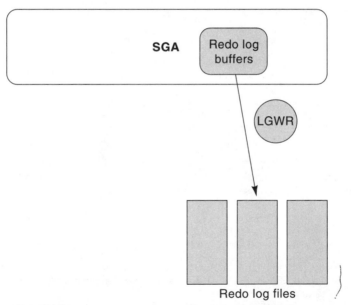

FIGURE 4.3 The LGWR writes data from the redo log buffer to redo log files.

Ordinarily, LGWR performs this task whenever a user completes a transaction, which happens when the user issues a COMMIT statement. This statement, which indicates that a transaction is complete, tells LGWR to copy the transaction's redo entries to a log file. Doing a write to disk each time a user issues a COMMIT results in one I/O operation for every COMMIT statement.

Sometimes this default behavior is not optimal. When many transactions are happening in a short period, handling them one at a time creates a backlog for LGWR. To prevent such a backlog, LGWR uses *group commit:* it writes the redo information for all the transactions at once. Doing so is faster than handling one transaction at a time because only one I/O operation is required for several COMMIT statements.

CKPT: Checkpoint process

To understand what this process does, you must understand the term *checkpoint*. A checkpoint is the moment the DBWR writes all modified database buffers—the buffers on the dirty list—to the data files. A checkpoint marks the point at which data gets saved to disk, so that in case of a failure, only transactions that occurred since the last checkpoint need to be recovered.

CKPT is the process that makes checkpoints work. CKPT triggers DBWR to write the contents of the *dirty list* (discussed in the special section "How the Server Uses the Database Buffer Cache") to data files. CKPT then puts a time stamp on the headers of the data files, so that during recovery it's clear when the last checkpoint occurred.

While the function performed by CKPT is critical, CKPT itself is optional because its role is performed by LGWR by default. However, if you have many data files, then timestamping the files could bog down LGWR. In such situations, you might want to enable CKPT.

SMON: System Monitor

You might want to think of SMON as the janitor of the background processes. Among other housekeeping tasks, SMON flushes out temporary segments that are no longer needed and consolidates contiguous free extents to enable the creation of larger segments.

PMON: Process Monitor

While SMON monitors the system—particularly the use of disk space—PMON monitors individual processes, including user processes and the server processes. If it finds a process that has died, it frees up resources that the process was using, and then restarts it.

ARCH: Archiver

The Archiver copies complete redo log files to disk or to some other permanent storage medium. (Figure 4.4)

The reason ARCH is useful is that redo log files eventually get overwritten. For example, if you have two redo log files and they both get filled up, LGWR will begin writing to the first one again, overwriting the file's previous redo entries. ARCH, in contrast, never overwrites the contents of the archive log files; ARCH just creates more archive log files as it stores entries from more and more redo logs. In other words, ARCH keeps a complete history of all transactions for a database.

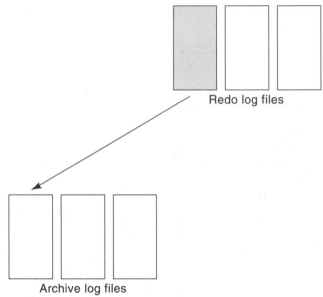

Redo log files

Archive log files

FIGURE 4.4   The ARCH copies data from filled redo log files to archive log files.

This way, if a disk containing a data file gets destroyed, you can recover all its data—even if the online redo log files don't have a complete record of all the transactions made after your last backup.

ARCH is optional: it only works if you have enabled archiving. But if you want to protect against media failure, then using ARCH is the only way.

RECO: Recoverer

One of the more complicated processes, RECO is responsible for resolving failures involving distributed transactions—that is, transactions that consist of SQL statements issued to tables located on different machines.

D*nnn*: Dispatcher processes

The *Dispatcher processes* are the intermediaries between user processes and server processes. When a user process issues a request, the dispatcher takes the request and puts it in a request queue. When the request reaches the head of the queue, the server process fulfills the request and returns the response to a dispatcher through the dispatcher's response queue.

Before Version 7 of the Oracle Server, there was no dispatcher process: each user process had a dedicated server process, so a process for matching up user processes with available server processes was unnecessary. Dispatcher processes became necessary when Version 7 introduced the multithreaded server, which allows for the existence of more user processes than server processes.

The *nnn* refers to the dispatcher's number.

LCK*n*: Lock processes

This process manages inter-instance locking. It is only used in a parallel server configuration.

STORING INFORMATION FOR A PROCESS

Whenever a server process or background process starts, part of memory gets allocated for storing information about the process. This area is called the *Program Global Area* or PGA. Unlike the SGA—in which the data is shared by several users—the PGA is a non-shared area. Because each process has its own PGA, the PGA is sometimes called the Private Global Area.

FILES

As noted earlier, a database consists of three types of files, all of which must be present for the database to work.

DATA FILES

The data of the logical structures—of tables, views, indexes, and other structures discussed in the previous chapter—are physically stored in the database's *data files*. Like other operating-system files, data files store information that can be read, changed, or protected from access.

But Oracle's data files are not merely operating-system files: the Oracle Server provides much finer control to what users can do to those files. Consider security. On a typical operating system, a user has some combination of read and write permission to particular files. A user with write permission to the file can change any part of it, and can even delete the file altogether. An Oracle user, on the other hand, can be restricted to modifying just part of the file. In fact, as you will see later, the Oracle Server does not use files at all to implement security; instead, it uses the logical structures. Similarly, the Server's lock management works on a finer level of granularity than the file level.

What is the exact relationship between the data files and the logical structures that the data files store? The relationship is most clear in the case of a tablespace: one or more data files correspond to a tablespace. As a result, a single schema object—such as an index—often gets stored in several data files. (Figure 4.5)

But while a logical structure can span more than one physical file, it cannot span more than one tablespace. A single table, for example, always resides in just one tablespace.

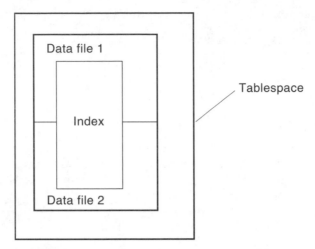

FIGURE 4.5   A schema object such as an index can be stored on more than one data file.

An important idea to keep in mind is that data files do not always contain the latest data. As noted earlier, DBWR doesn't write to the data files each time a user makes a change. Instead, the Server pools the data in memory until it determines that it makes sense to write the data to disk. But because DBWR's timeout interval is 3 seconds, the data files are never more than 3 seconds' worth of transactions behind the buffer cache.

Using Raw Files

On UNIX systems, you can use raw files—sometimes called raw devices or raw disk partitions—to store your data. Bypassing the UNIX file system in this way generally speeds up queries and updates because data can move directly between the raw file and the SGA. In other words, data does not get buffered by the UNIX kernel as it would if it were on regular files.

Using raw files, though, may not be the best strategy for every UNIX-based database system. Implementing raw files requires more operating-system expertise than using regular files; also, raw files require a more complex backup procedure than do standard files. Before choosing to use raw files, you need to consider whether your database's transaction volume is high enough to justify the increased system-administration overhead.

REDO LOG FILES

A database's *redo log files* store the log of all the changes made to the database. This log is known as the *redo log*. (Figure 4.6)

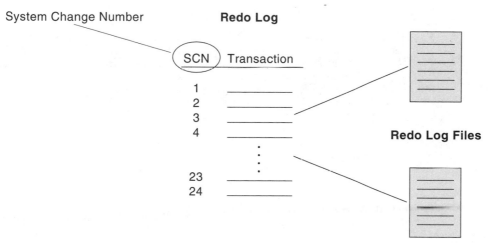

FIGURE 4.6 The transaction log is stored on two or more redo log files.

Knowing that the Server does not instantly write information to a data file, you can appreciate the importance of the redo log. Without a redo log, all records of transactions that are in memory when a system failure occurs disappear. Should a failure occur when there is a redo log, though, the Server can update the data files—recover the database—using the redo log files.

CONTROL FILES

A database's control file keeps track of the physical structure of the database. Among other items, it stores the physical locations of the data files and redo log files. The Server automatically changes the control file when a physical change in the database occurs. For example, when you create an additional data file, the Server notes the new filename and location in the control file.

This type of information is critical during recovery. It tells the Server from which log file to begin applying redo entries, where to find that file, and where to find the data files.

In this sense, the control file resembles a paper you might keep in your home which lists all the valuables in your wallet and phone numbers associated with those items: if your wallet gets lost or stolen, you can cancel all your credit cards and get new ones. Without this list, you might take a long time contacting all the credit-card companies or you might even forget about some cards completely.

Of course, only a very organized person keeps a list like this. To keep a control file, however, you don't have to do anything special except to back it up. The Oracle Server updates the control file automatically. In fact, because control files are binary files, only the Oracle Server can modify them. No person—including the DBA—should try to edit a control file.

HOW THE SERVER USES THE DATABASE BUFFER CACHE

The buffers in the database buffer cache are primarily organized into two lists: the *LRU list* and the *dirty list*.

TYPES OF BUFFERS

To see how these lists work, you must understand the types of buffers stored in the database buffer cache. There are items that are on neither list, but this consideration is not important to our discussion.

Free buffers

Free buffers are those that contain only data that has not been changed since it reached the buffer cache. For example, if you execute a query, bringing data from disk into the buffer cache, the data sits in the form of a free buffer until somebody updates it.

These buffers are called free because they are available for storing newer data: putting new data into them will not overwrite data that has not been saved to disk.

Dirty buffers

Dirty buffers are the opposite of free buffers: they contain data that has been modified since it reached the buffer cache. As a result, data in dirty buffers is different from corresponding data that is on disk. For example, a data file may indicate that the salary for PICARD is 52000, but the dirty buffer says that PICARD's salary is 55000. The dirty buffer reflects the update for PICARD's raise.

As you can see, *dirty* in this sense does not imply inaccurate. On the contrary, dirty buffers contain the most up-to-date data.

Pinned buffers

Pinned buffers are those that are currently being accessed. A free buffer that gets pinned can become a dirty buffer if it was pinned for an update. If, instead, it was pinned for a query, it becomes free after the pin is released.

THE DIRTY LIST

The dirty list contains dirty buffers. It is from this list that DBWR copies data to the data files. After it does so, the dirty list becomes empty and thus the database buffer cache becomes clean: data in memory is in sync with the data in the data files.

THE LRU LIST

The LRU list contains primarily free buffers and pinned buffers. It also contains some dirty buffers, which eventually move to the dirty list.

The LRU list gets its name from the algorithm (Least Recently Used) by which it's formed. This algorithm makes sure that the newest (most recently used) buffers remain at the head of the list while older (least recently used) buffers move toward the bottom of the list. (Figure 4.7)

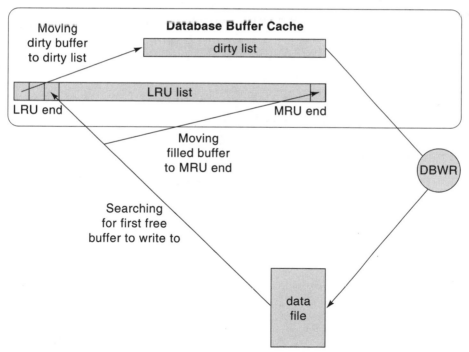

FIGURE 4.7 How the Server works with the LRU list and the dirty list.

Here's how this works.

When you issue a query, the Oracle Server tries to get the data from the buffer cache. If the data is in the cache, the Server does not have to go to disk. If the data is not in the cache, it reads the necessary data blocks from one of the data files and puts them in the first free buffers it encounters, starting at the LRU end of the list. (The reason it starts looking at the LRU end is that the buffers at that end, being old, are not as likely to contain data that users will need. If users do need this data, they can still get it from disk, though of course that will be slower than getting the data directly from the buffer cache.) Once the Server finds a free buffer, though, it copies the block into the buffer and moves the buffer to the Most Recently Used (MRU) end of the list. (This way, the new data is available until the buffer falls off the list, which does not happen until newer buffers push it to the LRU end.)

In searching for a free buffer, the Server may come across some pinned buffers and some dirty buffers. If it comes across a pinned buffer, it skips it. If it comes across a dirty buffer, it does not want to overwrite it because the data in that buffer is different from data that is on disk; therefore, the Server moves the dirty buffer to the dirty list and continues its search for a free buffer.

Part II   ADMINISTRATION

DATA INTEGRITY

CHAPTER OVERVIEW

Now that you understand the architecture of the Oracle Server, you are ready to learn about database administration. The following chapters describe how the Server helps DBAs do their job and how it solves the problems that every relational database system must handle.

One of these problems is the topic of this chapter—how to make sure that data in the database conforms to various rules. The sections below discuss several types of conformance: domain integrity, entity integrity, and referential integrity. They also discuss how the Oracle Server helps the DBA enforce these types of integrity, including declarative and procedural methods. (Figure 5.1)

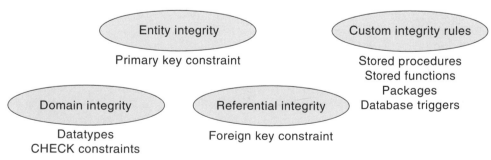

Entity integrity

Primary key constraint

Custom integrity rules

Stored procedures
Stored functions
Packages
Database triggers

Domain integrity

Datatypes
CHECK constraints

Referential integrity

Foreign key constraint

FIGURE 5.1   Types of data integrity and ways of enforcing them.

DOMAIN INTEGRITY AND DATATYPES

Perhaps the simplest type of integrity is domain integrity.

WHAT IS DOMAIN INTEGRITY?

Domain integrity for a column means that data in that column falls into the domain specified by the DBA. The domain includes the type of data (such as numbers or character strings) as well as the range of data. Domain integrity ensures that any value outside that domain is not allowed into the database.

For example, a domain might be all whole numbers between 1 and 300. If data integrity is being enforced, then users cannot enter the following values:

Value	Reason for Exclusion
doctor	incorrect datatype (CHAR instead of NUMBER)
2001	outside the range (not between 1 and 300)
27.5	outside the range (not a whole number)

The reason domain integrity is simple to maintain is that much of it is enforced automatically through datatypes. A DBA simply cannot create a new table without specifying a datatype—such as number or date—for each of the columns. Then, no matter what application a user uses to insert new data into your table, the user cannot insert data of a different datatype than the one you specified in defining your table.

Range checking, however, does not get enforced through datatypes. To have the Server check that a value entered by a user falls within a certain range, someone must specify the range. The easiest way to do this is to use a CHECK constraint, discussed later in this chapter.

WHY DOMAIN INTEGRITY?

An example will explain how domain integrity works and why it is important. Suppose you create a table LEADS for storing information about sales leads for your company's sales organization. Among other pieces of information, you want to store the date on which the salesperson last spoke with the lead. Since that date is not necessarily the date on which the sales assistant enters the data, the Server cannot enter it automatically. Instead, the assistant will need to enter the date manually, at the same that the assistant is entering other information (name, phone number, etc.)

If the Server does not enforce domain integrity, a user could enter information that would be difficult to retrieve later. For example, the sales assistant could make a typo and enter an invalid date—say, 13-29-95 instead of 12-29-95. Later, another user querying for all leads last contacted in December would not find this erroneous entry.

Using the correct datatype at table creation would prevent this problem. A *datatype*, which is an abstract description for the type of data that must occupy a particular column, guarantees that all data of that type fulfill certain requirements. Inherent in the DATE datatype, for example, is the rule that values for the month portion must be between 1 and 12.

THE DATATYPES

The following datatypes are available in Version 7 of the Oracle Server. Maximum lengths are specified in bytes rather than characters because Oracle supports many character-encoding schemes; in other words, a single character can correspond to one or several bytes, depending on which encoding scheme you choose.

NLS (National Language Support)

The Oracle Server is built for international use. Not only are error messages displayed in whatever language the DBA specifies, but the data entered by users can also be stored in the local language.

While English and other Indo-European languages—because of their short alphabets—can be encoded using just one byte per letter, Asian languages require several bytes to represent one character. Once you understand this, you can see why Oracle's column lengths are expressed in bytes, not characters.

CHAR

This fixed-length datatype is used for storing a string of characters, where a character is a letter, a digit, or a symbol such as a $. When you declare a column of type CHAR, you must specify the length. Then, when the user tries to enter data that exceeds that length, the Server reports an error. If the user enters a value that is shorter than the length specified by the DBA, the Server pads the extra spaces with blanks. The maximum length that you can declare is 255 bytes.

VARCHAR2

Like CHAR, VARCHAR2 is used for storing a string of characters. The difference is that a column declared as VARCHAR2 can store strings of varying lengths (though the maximum is 2000 bytes). Because the DBA only specifies the *maximum* length of a column of type VARCHAR2, the Server does not do any padding or truncation; instead, it stores the data exactly as entered.

VARCHAR

In Version 7, this datatype is identical to VARCHAR2. It exists only for possible future use. Consequently, for this release, Oracle Corporation recommends the use of VARCHAR2 instead of VARCHAR.

LONG

LONG is similar to VARCHAR2 because it stores variable-length character strings. As its name implies, though, it's intended for longer character strings. With the limit being two gigabytes, LONG is a good choice for storing large chunks of text—from an email message to an entire novel.

NUMBER

This datatype stores all types of numbers: the Oracle Server does not make a distinction between integers and real numbers. The idea is to simplify data access, so that users do not have to know how a number is actually stored in order to find its value or to enter a new value.

At the same time, while declaring a column to be of type NUMBER, you can specify the number's precision and scale. For example, you could issue the following statement:

```
CREATE TABLE gauss.types
      (specimen_id        NUMBER,
       temperature        NUMBER(8,2));
```

With this statement, you create a table owned by GAUSS containing two numerical columns. The first column simply stores an identifier. The second column stores the temperatures to eight significant digits, rounded to the second decimal place. You can see, then, that an Oracle database can be used to store and compute scientific data. In fact, Oracle numbers support up to 38 decimal digits of precision.

DATE

DATE actually stores both the date and the time of day, including seconds. As with other datatypes, users need not be concerned with the way the data is stored, the internal format.

However, it is useful to know the format in which dates must be entered. By default, the format for data entry and output is DD-MON-YY. This means that dates like "12-DEC-69" are allowed, while dates in other formats are not.

The Oracle Server does allow users, programmers, and DBAs to change the format for data entry. A DBA can change the default by changing the value of the initialization parameter NLS_DATE_FORMAT. For example, to have dates entered and displayed with the day preceding the month, the DBA can include the following entry in the initialization parameter file:

```
NLS_DATE_FORMAT = 'DD-MM-YY'
```

Similarly, the DBA can set the default way that hours and minutes are entered and displayed:

```
NLS_DATE_FORMAT = 'HH:MI-DD-MM-YY'
```

Users and programmers can override this default. Users can use the TO_DATE function when inserting, updating, or selecting rows, and programmers can define a format mask when coding an application. But regardless of how the date is entered or how it is displayed by a particular user or application, the date stored in the database is always stored in the same internal format by the Oracle Server. The DATE datatype thus preserves data integrity.

If dates are stored in a column whose datatype is DATE, the Oracle Server can perform date arithmetic on the data. For example, you could find all employees who have been with your company for more than two years by issuing the following SQL statement:

```
SQL> SELECT emp_id, last_name, first_name FROM org
  2  WHERE (SYSDATE - hire_date) > 730;
```

This example uses 730 because in date expressions, the Oracle Server interprets numerical constants as days. Because one year generally equals 365 days, we use 2 * 365 to represent two years.

RAW

This datatype stores binary data with a maximum length of 2000 bytes.

LONG RAW

With a maximum length of 2 gigabytes, this extension of RAW is good for storing large binary objects such as executable programs or large non-text documents, such as graphics files.

ROWID

This datatype is primarily used for one column in a table, namely the pseudocolumn called ROWID.

ROWID is a pseudocolumn because the data in it is derived from other information. Specifically, the ROWID is the physical address of the data block containing the first part of the row.

The datatype ROWID, then, is the format for this type of data. Internally, the values of ROWID are stored in binary format. To the user who issues a query involving ROWID, though, the values are presented in hexadecimal format. The parts of the hexadecimal string denote the block, row within the block, and data file containing the row.

For example, suppose you issue the following query:

```
SQL> SELECT student_id, rowid FROM students
  2  WHERE last_name = 'Smith';
```

You will get a result like the following:

```
STUDENT_ID          ROWID
------------------------------------
2812448             0000089D.0000.0001
2840972             0000089D.0001.0001
2362720             0000089D.0002.0001
8084563             0000089D.0003.0001
```

This output tells you that the rows for all four students named Smith are stored in the first data file and in the same block within the data file.

Because the pseudocolumn ROWID exists for every table and always has the datatype ROWID, you don't have to declare it.

ENTITY INTEGRITY AND THE PRIMARY KEY

While domain integrity is a property of individual columns, *entity integrity* is a property of a table. If a table has entity integrity, then for every row in the table, there is at least one statement that will fetch only that row. Therefore, a table that has entity integrity contains no duplicate rows.

To make sure that all tables in an Oracle database have this property, the Oracle Server prevents users from creating a table without specifying a *primary key* for the table. The primary key is the column or set of columns that uniquely identifies a particular row.

A simple example of a primary key is a column that stores a sequence. Since values in such a column get assigned sequentially, there are no duplicate values; therefore, querying the database by a particular number in the sequence guarantees that only one row will be returned.

In a database without a sequence, a primary key might be the LAST_NAME column, but only if there are no duplicate last names in the database. If there are, the primary key might have to be the pair of columns LAST_NAME and FIRST_NAME. In other words, only by querying by both the first name and the last name are you guaranteed to find the one individual for whom you are looking.

We will look at how to declare the PRIMARY KEY constraint in the "Using Declarative Integrity Constraints" section.

REFERENTIAL INTEGRITY AND THE FOREIGN KEY

The third type of data integrity, *referential integrity*, governs the data content in multiple tables. It guarantees that related tables are truly related; that is, that data in one column of a table matches the data in the corresponding column in the related table.

REFERENCING VERSUS REFERENCED TABLES

To understand referential integrity, it helps to know the terms *referencing table* and *referenced table*. A referencing table is one that refers to another table, the referenced table. The referenced table can stand on its own, but a referencing table always depends on another table.

For example, suppose a university has a table FACULTY which stores the employee ID and name of each professor. In addition, the COURSES table stores information about courses taught at the university. This information might include the course ID, course title, teacher, number of credits, and other such data. The relationship between the two tables is that every course in COURSES must be taught by someone listed in FACULTY. Therefore, FACULTY is the referenced table while COURSES is the referencing table.

Several other terms are synonymous: *master* and *parent* are synonymous with *referenced*, while *dependent* and *child* have the same meaning as *referencing*.

THE FOREIGN KEY

The column or set of columns in a referencing table that refers to the referenced table is called the *foreign key*. The foreign key corresponds to the referenced table's primary key or to a unique key. In our example, teacher_id in COURSES is the foreign key referencing employee_id in FACULTY. (Figure 5.2)

Referential integrity is in place when every value in a foreign key corresponds to a value in the primary key or a unique key. For example, if you can insert a row into COURSES with a teacher_id that does not exist in the employee_id column of FACULTY, then there is no referential integrity between those columns.

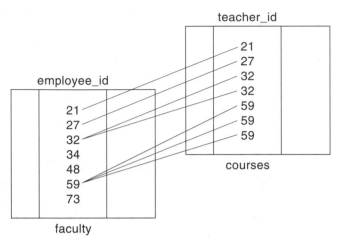

FIGURE 5.2 Every value in the foreign key of the referencing table, COURSES, corresponds to a value in the primary key of the referenced table, FACULTY. Therefore, referential integrity is in place between the two tables.

SELF-REFERENTIAL INTEGRITY

A special case of referential integrity is *self-referential integrity*. Self-referential integrity refers to a situation in which the primary key and the foreign key are in the same table.

A common example of self-referential integrity is an employee table, which we have called ORG. You will recall that among other data, ORG contains employee names and the names of their managers. But because managers are employees too,

FIGURE 5.3 An example of self-referential integrity.

their names appear not only in the manager column but in the LAST_NAME column, as well. Self-referential integrity ensures that every manager's name also appears in the LAST_NAME column. That is, MANAGER_LAST_NAME is the foreign key that corresponds to the LAST_NAME primary key. (Figure 5.3)

ENFORCING REFERENTIAL INTEGRITY

To enforce referential integrity, you must declare the FOREIGN KEY constraint when creating the referencing table. We will look at how to do this in the next section.

USING DECLARATIVE INTEGRITY CONSTRAINTS

So far, we have looked at the three types of data integrity. You have learned that domain integrity is enforced largely through datatypes, and that to enforce entity integrity and referential integrity, you must use *integrity constraints*.

To appreciate the value of the Oracle Server's integrity constraints, it helps to be aware that an alternative method of enforcing integrity rules exists: a programmer can code these rules into a client program. For example, an application used to enter course data could check user input and send an error message if the user enters a value for teacher_id that does not exist in the FACULTY table. But if several applications access a database, then this sort of coding becomes needlessly redundant. It makes more sense to specify the data integrity rules at the Server level. Allowing the programmer or DBA to do that is the idea behind integrity constraints.

The following sections describe the different types of declarative integrity constraints. These constraints are called "declarative" because they are declared (only once, during table creation). Thus, they stand in contrast to the programmatic constructs we will discuss in a later section.

As you read about the various integrity constraints, notice that some do more than ensure entity integrity and referential integrity. Using the integrity constraints of Oracle7, you can declare other specific rules for what type of data is allowed in your database.

NOT NULL

A NOT NULL constraint on a column of a table ensures that no null values are allowed in that column. A null value means that the value is undefined. For example, if no user has entered a salary for an employee and the SALARY column has no default value, then the value of SALARY is null.

To make sure that for every employee in the ORG table, a salary amount is listed, you must declare a NOT NULL constraint on the SALARY column of ORG:

```
CREATE TABLE org_a
       (.
         .
         .
       SALARY        NUMBER(12,2) NOT NULL);
```

With this NOT NULL constraint in place, a user cannot insert a row into ORG without specifying a value for SALARY. (Figure 5.4)

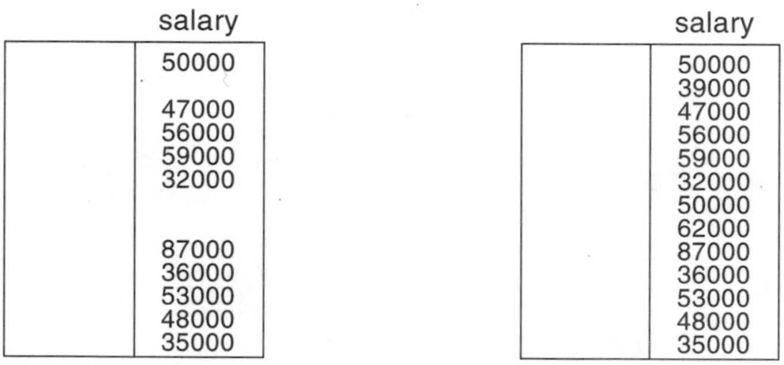

salary
50000
47000
56000
59000
32000
87000
36000
53000
48000
35000

ORG_A without constraint

salary
50000
39000
47000
56000
59000
32000
50000
62000
87000
36000
53000
48000
35000

ORG_A with NOT NULL constraint

FIGURE 5.4   Effect of a NOT NULL constraint.

You must declare this constraint because, by default, the Oracle Server allows null values in all columns.

Implicitly, a primary key is NOT NULL because each value in the primary key column is unique. (An explicitly declared UNIQUE constraint, however, does not prevent column values from being null.) If null values were permitted in a column, it would be possible to have more than one row with a null value. Therefore, the column would cease to serve as the primary key.

UNIQUE

While a primary key is always UNIQUE and NOT NULL, other columns can be made UNIQUE for other reasons. An obvious reason is that you want to avoid redundant data, but do want to allow null values.

You can declare a UNIQUE constraint on one column or on several columns. To force one column to be unique (Figure 5.5), you create a column-level constraint like the kind we have already seen:

```
CREATE TABLE org_b
       (.
         .
         .
       last_name   VARCHAR2(20)        UNIQUE);
```

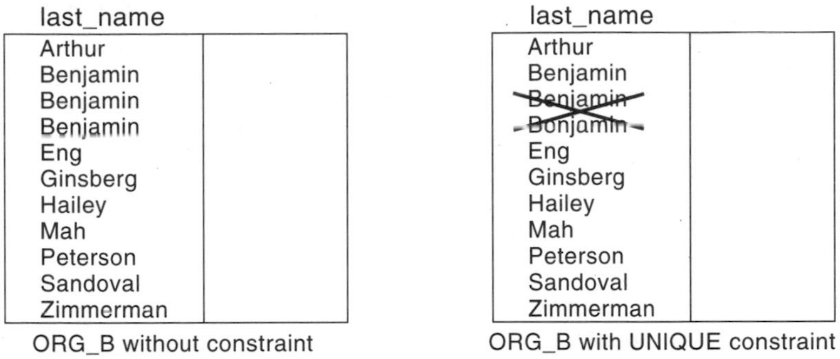

FIGURE 5.5 Effect of a UNIQUE constraint.

But suppose that it's acceptable to have two or more people with the same last name. What you don't want is more than one person with the same first and last names. To prevent having two Judy Lermans, you need to create a composite UNIQUE key constraint:

```
CREATE TABLE org_c
     (.
      first_name  VARCHAR2(20),
      last_name   VARCHAR2(20),
      CONSTRAINT uniq_empname
           UNIQUE (first_name,last_name));
```

Notice that in this example, the constraint gets explicitly declared with the CONSTRAINT keyword and a constraint name. Because it consists of two columns, it gets declared at the end of the entire CREATE TABLE statement rather than after a single column definition.

Of course, you might have two or more employees with the same first and last name working in your company. If this is the case, the above UNIQUE constraint would cause problems. It would be more appropriate to define a UNIQUE constraint on more than just those two columns, so that the rule you're enforcing is that the combination of first name, middle name, last name, and date of birth must be unique.

PRIMARY KEY

To tell the Server which column or columns of a table should be the primary key, you must use the PRIMARY KEY constraint. If you want to make just one column the primary key, declare a column-level constraint:

```
CREATE TABLE faculty_a
     (employee_id       NUMBER       PRIMARY KEY,
      .
      .
      .);
```

After a table is created with this constraint, users cannot insert rows that either have duplicate or null values for the employee_id column.

To create a primary key on two columns, use a table-level constraint:

```
CREATE TABLE faculty_b
     ( .
       first_name VARCHAR2(20),
       last_name  VARCHAR2(20),
       CONSTRAINT pk_faculty
           PRIMARY KEY (first_name,last_name));
```

By declaring this composite primary key, you are forcing users to enter values for both first_name and last_name. Thus, a primary key constraint enforces not only the UNIQUE constraint but also the NOT NULL constraint.

FOREIGN KEY

Like the PRIMARY KEY constraint, the FOREIGN KEY constraint gets declared at table creation. To use the foreign constraint, however, you must have already created the referenced table—unless, of course, you are creating a self-referencing table.

Basic Syntax Example

For example, after creating the table faculty_a, you can create a child table that references it:

```
CREATE TABLE courses_a
     ( .
       .
       teacher_id NUMBER              REFERENCES faculty_a,
     .);
```

Notice that in this example, the keyword REFERENCES (with a table name as an argument) is enough to indicate that teacher_id is the foreign key which references the primary key in faculty_a. This is because faculty_a, like any table, can have at most one primary key.

When to Specify the Referenced Column Name

If, however, teacher_id referenced not the primary key but simply a unique key of faculty_a, then the argument to REFERENCES would have to specify the referenced column name, as in the following fragment:

```
teacher_id NUMBER       REFERENCES faculty_a (column name)
```

In both of the above examples, the keyword FOREIGN KEY is implied because the word REFERENCES immediately follows the column name of the foreign key.

When to Use the FOREIGN KEY Keyword

Sometimes, though, you may need to define the foreign key at the table level, as we've done on composite UNIQUE and PRIMARY KEY constraints:

```
CREATE TABLE courses_b
    ( .
    first_name VARCHAR2(20),
    last_name  VARCHAR2(20),
    CONSTRAINT fk_courses
        FOREIGN KEY (first_name,last_name)
        REFERENCES faculty_b (first_name,last_name));
```

Here, the FOREIGN KEY keyword is necessary to specify which columns comprise the foreign key.

Using the ON DELETE CASCADE Option

Creating a FOREIGN KEY constraint establishes a dependent relationship between the referenced table and the referencing table. Deleting a row in the master table could cause a problem with referential data integrity. For example, if a faculty member leaves the university and her row gets deleted from the FACULTY table, what happens to the courses she was assigned to teach? Keeping her teacher_id in the COURSES table would violate the FOREIGN KEY constraint we have defined, because there would be a value in the teacher_id column of the dependent table that did not correspond to a value in the employee_id column of the master table.

In reality, this violation could not occur because the Oracle Server enforces integrity constraints. But how does the Oracle Server deal with such a situation? What does it do when a user tries to delete a row containing a value referenced by another table?

Depending on how the FOREIGN KEY constraint was defined, the Oracle Server can either:

❏ forbid the deletion of any rows in the parent table that are referenced in the child table

❏ allow the row in the parent table to be deleted, and then delete all dependent rows in the child table

By default, the Oracle Server uses the former strategy to maintain referential integrity. It will use the latter strategy only if the FOREIGN KEY constraint was declared with the ON DELETE CASCADE option.

For example, to make sure all courses taught by a teacher who is no longer listed in table faculty_a get deleted from courses_a, you must use the following syntax:

```
CREATE TABLE courses_a
      (.
       .
       teacher_id NUMBER        REFERENCES faculty_a
                                ON DELETE CASCADE,
      .);
```

If you omit the ON DELETE CASCADE option, then an employee row cannot be deleted from faculty_a if any rows in courses_a reference it.

CHECK

A CHECK constraint lets you further limit the values in a column. For example, suppose you want to make sure that all values of the DAY column are valid abbreviations for the days of the week. For you, this means that they are in the set {SUN, MON, TUE, WED, THU, FRI, SAT}. You can use a CHECK constraint to ensure just that:

```
CREATE TABLE check_a
      (.
       .
       day  CHAR(3)        CHECK (day IN ('SUN','MON','TUE',
                                  'WED','THU','FRI','SAT')),
      .);
```

The user who accidentally enters MOM instead of MON will get an error. Your CHECK constraint will have effectively maintained the integrity of the data in column DAY.

For columns of type NUMBER, a CHECK constraint can ensure that all values are within a particular range.

```
CREATE TABLE check_b
      (.
       .
       code NUMBER  CHECK (code BETWEEN 1000 AND 4000),
      .);
```

The above constraint ensures that all values for the CODE column are between 1000 and 4000, so that numbers like 924 and 6000 are not allowed.

You can also use a CHECK constraint to allow values in a column only if a condition about some *other* columns in the same table is true. For example, suppose you want the Oracle Server to enforce the rule that only exempt employees get bonuses. You might use the following syntax:

```
CREATE TABLE org
    (.
     status      CHAR(3)     CHECK (status IN 'EXM', 'NON'),
     bonus       NUMBER(8,2) CHECK (status = 'EXM'),
     .);
```

With this constraint in place, the Oracle Server will allow a non-null value in the BONUS column only if the value in the STATUS column indicates that the employee is exempt.

ENFORCING CUSTOM DATA INTEGRITY RULES USING PROCEDURAL MEANS

Using the relational model, some business rules may remain unenforced even though domain integrity, entity integrity, and referential integrity are in place. To enforce special business rules that cannot be enforced declaratively, Oracle provides several procedural constructs: stored procedures, functions, packages, and database triggers.

With these constructs, you gain the programming flexibility that you might enjoy by writing custom applications. At the same time, by using stored procedures, database triggers, and other subroutines, you centralize the enforcement of data integrity. This way, when business rules governing a particular database change, you do not have to change every application that accesses the database.

Using these Server subroutines also improves database performance. Because the entire subroutine is stored in compiled form in the database, it does not have to be recompiled each time it's called. Also, network traffic between the client and the server consists only of procedure and function calls, not of entire chunks of actual code.

STORED PROCEDURES, FUNCTIONS, AND PACKAGES

Data-integrity rules that need to apply to the whole database but cannot be enforced using the declarative integrity constraints can be enforced using *stored procedures* and *stored functions*. Stored procedures and functions are blocks of pre-compiled PL/SQL code which are stored in the Data Dictionary. The main difference between a procedure and a function is that a function always returns a value. When a client needs to execute one of these blocks, all it needs to do is to send a procedure call and the required parameters. (Figure 5.6)

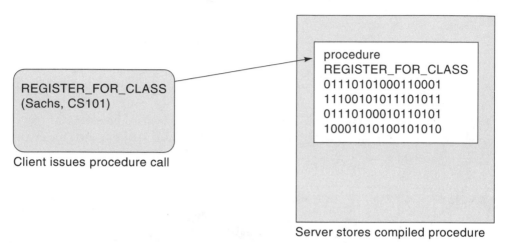

Client issues procedure call

Server stores compiled procedure

FIGURE 5.6 Calling stored procedures from a client application.

A *package* is simply a set of stored procedures, functions, and other program objects (such as variables and constants) that gets executed as a single entity. (Figure 5.7)

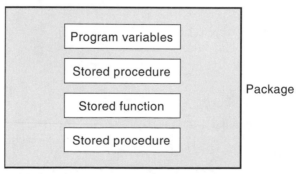

FIGURE 5.7 A package consists of stored procedures, functions, and other PL/SQL objects.

Suppose you are automating the class enrollment process in a university. The registrar's office was using computers before for registering students for classes at the beginning of each quarter, but the registrar was manually entering the information one field at a time. This process not only took a long time, but it left room for errors to creep in. For example, students would enroll in classes with overlapping meeting periods. Or they would register for classes for which they had not met the prerequisites.

What do you do to solve these problems? One solution is to create a package called REGISTER_STUDENT. To register a student, the registrar would execute the package, entering the values for the package's parameters. The package would do the rest: for each course for which the student requested enrollment, it would call a stored procedure called REGISTER_FOR_CLASS which would check the COURSES table to make sure the class was not yet filled. REGISTER_STUDENT might call other procedures, such as CHECK_PREREQUISITES, CHECK_TIMES, and, at the end, CHECK_UNITS, to make sure the total courseload did not exceed the university's maximum.

This sort of checking—taking into account values stored in multiple tables—cannot be performed by a CHECK constraint. PL/SQL code, on the other hand, is ideally suited to the enforcement of these complex rules.

DATABASE TRIGGERS

A *database trigger* is a special type of stored procedure, one that fires when a user makes a change to the data in a database. Depending on how you write the trigger, it will fire when one of the following commands is executed: UPDATE, INSERT, or DELETE. A trigger is so called because its execution gets triggered by some event in the database, not by an explicit user call (as is the case with stored procedures, functions, and packages).

Suppose, for example, that you have an inventory database. Since you want to make sure you minimize stockouts, you want an alert to fire whenever the quantity-on-hand for a particular part reaches a certain point. This reorder point is not the same for all parts, but varies by usage. In other words, rather than being a constant, the re-order point can best be expressed as a formula—in terms of the part's usage and delivery time.

Clearly, such rules are too complex to implement using declarative integrity constraints. Nor will a simple stored procedure do the job, because somebody needs to know when to call it. But because the information needed to make the calculation for reaching the decision (to fire an alert or not) can easily be stored in a database, you can use PL/SQL to write a trigger that fires when a user updates a value in the quantity column.

DATA CONSISTENCY
AND CONCURRENCY

CHAPTER OVERVIEW

In this chapter, we continue our exploration of how the Oracle Server makes sure data is correct. While most scenarios we have considered thus far are fairly simple in that they rely on one user per database, here we turn to the more common, real-world of multiple users simultaneously, or *concurrently*, accessing a single database.

The problems of this scenario are clear. Imagine several agents in a city selling tickets to a popular play or concert. It's easy to picture two or more of them making a simultaneous sales transaction. Since the number of tickets is limited, how do you make sure that several agents don't sell the same ticket?

After introducing some relevant terms, we discuss how the Oracle Server solves this classic problem in keeping data consistent when multiple concurrent users are writing to the same database. Then we turn to another data consistency problem, one that involves users who read from a database while others write to it. The goal in both these problems, and hence the title of this chapter, is to achieve maximum concurrency (large number of simultaneous users) while maintaining perfect consistency (correct data).

STATEMENTS AND TRANSACTIONS

First, it's important to clarify some terminology. A *statement*, as noted earlier, is a single SQL command, which can range from a simple UPDATE, INSERT, or SELECT statement to a complex SQL command involving several clauses (such as a SELECT statement with WHERE and ORDER BY clauses). You can think of a SQL statement as one or more clauses followed by a semicolon.

A *transaction*, in contrast, can consist of either one or multiple SQL statements issued by a single user or application. The duration of a transaction depends solely on the point at which the user or application issues a COMMIT. (Figure 6.1) While the Server does write uncommitted data to data files, it makes certain that such an incomplete transaction can be rolled back. In rollback segments, it stores the previous values of all modified rows. In redo log files, it only stores entries for transactions that have been committed. This way, if a user issues a ROLLBACK statement or if the transaction aborts because of a failure, the Server can roll back all the uncommitted changes and thus bring the database back to its previous state.

```
DELETE FROM org                DELETE FROM org
WHERE emp_id = 15270;          WHERE emp_id = 15270;

                               INSERT INTO org
                               VALUES 10732, 'Wu', 'Sally';

                               COMMIT;
```

             Statement   **Transaction**

FIGURE 6.1   A statement ends with a semicolon.
A transaction ends with a COMMIT statement.

When we say that two transactions are *concurrent*, we don't necessarily mean that they started and ended at the same time. Even when transactions merely overlap, there is the potential for one of them to interfere with the other. Therefore, the statements are said to be concurrent.

Why is all of this important? The reason is that true concurrency poses problems such as the one described in the chapter overview. The basic way of getting around these problems is to treat concurrent processes as if they were happening serially—one after the other. The test of whether data is consistent during concurrent processing, after all, is whether the data is the same as it would be if the two or more processes occurred one after the other. And the best way to serialize actions while continuing to provide access to many users is to break these actions into small, well-defined chunks: SQL statements and transactions.

ENSURING ACCURATE WRITES

As we suggested in the overview to this chapter, one danger of having multiple users write to the same database is that one user can impact the work of another user.

Here's how this could happen.

THE LOST-UPDATE PROBLEM

The database starts out with 20 tickets remaining for the concert. The first ticket agent, Jodie, sells three tickets and makes the update in the database. Before this update gets committed, another agent, Fred, sells two tickets. Fred's processor subtracts two from the current value in the database—still 20—and gets 18. Meanwhile, Jodie's value (17) gets written to disk. A second later, Fred's value (18) gets written to disk. The effect of Jodie's sale thus gets overwritten. Even though there are only 15 tickets left, the database says that there are still 18 tickets available.

Clearly, this result is unacceptable. In our example, it would lead to more tickets sold than seats available, and there are many similar problems in the real world. If many users have uncontrolled access to the same items, inventory records can easily get corrupted. The potential problem with financial data is even more severe: whereas the numbers in an inventory database correspond to physical entities and can be confirmed by taking a physical inventory, numbers in a financial database don't always represent a physical entity. If inconsistencies arise in a bank, it's impossible to go to the vault and see how many dollar bills are actually in someone's account!

HOW LOCKS PREVENT DESTRUCTIVE INTERFERENCE

In any case, all these problems, which stem from interference between two or more processes modifying the same item, are unacceptable in a database management system. To prevent this sort of destructive interference, the Oracle Server and other database systems use locks.

What Is a Lock?

In the physical world, a lock is a mechanism that controls access. In the database world, and in software in general, a *lock* is a mechanism that prevents some form of access to an entity that is being used by another user or application.

For example, suppose you and a coworker both have Write permission to a text file, and your co-worker, Sam, is currently making edits to the file. When you open the file to make your own changes, you get a message that the file is locked by user SAM. You cannot view or edit the file because either the operating system or the editor has put a lock on the file.

Oracle's Lock Manager

While multiuser operating systems—such as many of those on which the Oracle Server runs—have a lock manager that controls and maintains locks, the Oracle Server does not rely on it. Instead, it has its own system for managing locks, one that works the same way regardless of the underlying operating system.

The advantage of having Oracle control the locking is not only in portability. Although consistent behavior across hardware platforms is a goal of the Oracle Server, the greatest benefit of having the Server control locking is that it can provide a more sophisticated lock manager than any single operating system. The Server's lock manager both provides finer granularity and chooses the optimal level of granularity for a particular situation.

With rare exceptions, which we will consider at the end of the chapter, a programmer does not have to apply locks. The Server automatically applies locks when necessary, choosing the right lock for each situation.

Using the Right Lock for Maximum Concurrency

Think back to the file-editing example. Suppose that instead of making any changes, you only wanted to look at the file that Sam is editing. Since viewing the file would not pose the risk that you might overwrite Sam's work, you see no reason why you should be not be allowed to view the file. And you would be right. If the application did not allow you even to view the file, it would be too careful about data consistency—it would be providing data consistency at the cost of concurrency.

Striking the optimal balance between providing maximum concurrent access while maintaining consistent data is what a good lock manager does. One way it does so is by using different types of locks, depending on what a particular situation requires. These locks vary by both their *restrictiveness* and by their *granularity*.

LOCK RESTRICTIVENESS

The restrictiveness, or exclusivity, of a lock determines the number of people or processes that have access to the item locked.

Exclusive Locks

An *exclusive lock* on an item (such as on a row) prevents all other transactions from obtaining locks on that item. Note that this does not mean that other transactions cannot access the item. For example, if a transaction only contains SELECT statements, it can access the locked item because a SELECT does not lock an item.

With the Oracle Server, a lock on a row is always an exclusive lock.

Share Locks

A *share lock* on an item is, as its name implies, less restrictive than an exclusive lock; it allows other transactions to lock the item using another share lock, but it prevents locking with an exclusive lock. In our file-editing example, when Sam opens up the text file, the system might put a share lock on the file so that other users could read the file but not write to it.

Clearly, share locks allow more transactions to occur concurrently. While row locks are always exclusive, a table lock can be in any of five modes, or levels of restrictiveness. For the purposes of this book, it's not necessary to know the modes; all you need to understand is that different statements trigger table locks of different modes, and that a lock of a less restrictive mode prevents other transactions from acquiring locks of a more restrictive mode.

The more restrictive the lock, the less concurrency. Therefore, to maximize concurrency, the Server automatically uses the least restrictive lock necessary to prevent destructive interference.

LOCK GRANULARITY

The granularity of a lock determines the fineness of the item locked. The smaller the item locked, the finer the granularity. The larger the item locked, the coarser the granularity is said to be. In the case of Sam and his file, the granularity is coarse because no matter how small a change Sam is making, the entire file gets locked.

Row Locks

A row lock locks only the row being modified. Row-level locking is important when many users are accessing the same table, because such locking allows users to continue to modify data in the rest of the table.

Contrast row locking to block-level locking, which the Oracle Server does not use. With block-level locking, the entire data block containing the row being modified gets locked. Thus, if a block contains two rows—only one of which is being modified—the block-level lock would prevent both rows from being modified by another user. If a row is spread over three blocks, and each block contains one other row, then block-level locking would cause a total of four rows from being modified, instead of just the one being modified.

Yet despite the advantage of row-level locking over block-level locking, row-level locking is not available in all relational database systems. In fact, other than the Oracle Server, Informix is the only commercial relational database system to provide this feature.

Table Locks

A table lock is a lock on the entire table; when a transaction obtains a table lock, no other transaction can—depending on the lock's restrictiveness—perform actions on the entire table. A table lock, then, is of a coarser granularity than a row lock.

When does a transaction obtain a table lock? It does so when a table is being changed. In fact, whenever a transaction obtains a row lock, it obtains a table lock as well, though the table lock is less restrictive.

Why does the Server enable a table lock if there is already a row lock on the affected row? It's important to understand that the purposes behind a row lock and the corresponding table lock are different. The purpose of a row lock is to prevent other statements from modifying a row being modified by the statement that acquires the lock. The purpose of a table lock, in contrast, is to make sure that the DBA cannot change the definition of the table—altering the table's integrity constraints, for example—until the data-manipulation transaction has been committed.

Even though the Oracle Server does use table locks, such locks do not prevent users from issuing INSERT, UPDATE, DELETE, or SELECT statements. The only way that an Oracle table lock will prevent a DML operation is if you are using manual locking, explicitly issuing a LOCK command with a very restrictive mode. The Server's automatic locking behavior is not that restrictive. Each transaction acquires the least-restrictive lock necessary to prevent destructive interference, so that many concurrent users can enter data with a minimal period of waiting for locks to be released.

HOW THE SERVER HANDLES LOCKS

When a transaction contains a DML statement other than SELECT, the transaction acquires an exclusive row lock on the row being modified. It also acquires a table lock that prevents DDL operations to the table being modified.

In the following statement, the transaction acquires an exclusive lock on the row in which EMP_ID is 11460:

```
SQL> UPDATE org
  2  SET manager = 'Chapman'
  3  WHERE emp_id = 11460;
```

Thus, other users cannot update or delete the row. (Figure 6.2) (Users can, however, select the row, as we will see in the next section.) Furthermore, the entire table ORG gets locked against such DDL operations as dropping or altering the table.

In the next statement, the transaction acquires an exclusive lock on several rows:

```
SQL> DELETE FROM stock
  2  WHERE part_id < 300;
```

Deadlocks

A *deadlock* is a situation in which two or more transactions cannot proceed because each is waiting for the other to release a lock.

For example, suppose Lauren and Richard have joint checking and savings accounts. Lauren needs to transfer $2,000 from savings so that she has enough in checking to make a mortgage payment.

Meanwhile, Richard wants to transfer the $1,500 currently in the checking account to savings, so that the money can earn some interest. Each spouse's transaction consists of two statements, each of which takes fractions of a second.

Richard's are:
  1. UPDATE checking   time = 0:00:01
  2. UPDATE savings   time = 0:00:03

Lauren's are:
  1. UPDATE savings   time = 0:00:00
  2. UPDATE checking   time = 0:00:02

The times indicate when each statement begins.

You can probably anticipate the problem. Lauren starts first. Her transaction locks their savings account's row and will not release the lock until checking has been incremented. But checking cannot be touched because by now Richard has begun a transaction that locked the couple's checking account row. Richard, of course, cannot end the transaction and release the lock on checking because of Lauren's lock on savings. Lauren and Richard are in a deadlock.

As we have said, a database system must allow several users to work concurrently with as little delay caused by locks as possible. A deadlock is a serious failure of concurrent processing because neither user can continue work at all, never mind how fast.

How does the Oracle Server get out of this situation? It uses rollbacks. Once it notices that a deadlock is in place, it rolls back the transaction that detects the deadlock, thus releasing the first lock. As a result, the second transaction can proceed (allowing the user to COMMIT). Once the second user commits, the first user can proceed as well.

In general, though, the Server's design makes deadlocks rare to begin with. The probability of a deadlock is low because the Server uses row-level locking instead of a coarser level of locking and because statements that merely read data do not acquire locks at all.

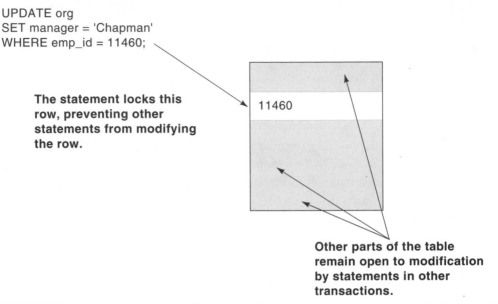

```
UPDATE org
SET manager = 'Chapman'
WHERE emp_id = 11460;
```

The statement locks this row, preventing other statements from modifying the row.

11460

Other parts of the table remain open to modification by statements in other transactions.

FIGURE 6.2 A row lock prevents other transactions from modifying the row, but allows modifications to other rows in the table.

Suppose there are 15 rows that fit the condition that the part number be less than 300. In this case, each of the 15 rows gets locked. If no rows fit the condition, then no rows get locked because no modification occurs. In addition, the table STOCK gets a lock that prevents destructive DDL operations.

A special kind of SELECT statement—SELECT ... FOR UPDATE—also acquires locks. A user or application issues a SELECT ... FOR UPDATE statement in order to see values before updating them or before deleting rows that contain them. For example, if a user wants to see which rows in the STOCK table correspond to parts with a quantity of 0 before deleting those rows, she could enter the following statement:

```
SQL> SELECT part_id, description
  2   FROM stock
  3   WHERE qty = 0
  4   FOR UPDATE;
```

The user wants to make sure that before deleting the result set, values in the rows do not change. (If she does not care if the values change after she looks, then she can issue a simple SELECT statement, which does not acquire locks.) By issuing a SELECT ... FOR UPDATE, she locks all the selected rows against updates by other users. Then, if she is satisfied with the result set, she can issue her DELETE statement using the same WHERE clause, confident that she will delete the same rows that she selected.

The locks acquired by all these statements get held until the transaction—not the statement—ends. When the user or application issues a COMMIT statement, the transaction ends successfully and releases all the locks it held. (Even if the transaction ends unsuccessfully—if it gets rolled back—the locks get released.) As a result, other users can modify any part of the table, and DBAs can make structural changes to the table. Of course by this time, another transaction may have acquired locks on other rows, thus preventing modification to those rows and preventing DBAs from dropping or altering the table. Nonetheless, you can see that this row-level locking allows for maximum concurrency because many INSERT, DELETE, and UPDATE statements can do their work simultaneously, so long as they are not accessing the same rows.

ENSURING ACCURATE READS

In the previous section, you learned that the Oracle Server locks a row modified by a transaction. Furthermore, as mentioned above, those Oracle Server transactions that contain only SELECT statements do not acquire locks. This makes sense because users who want to modify or query data should not have to wait for users who are only reading data, not modifying. Because there is no chance of destructive interference in such cases, the Oracle Server allows concurrent transactions to continue.

These scenarios, however, only cover part of the story. They describe what happens when one transaction modifies data, and they show what happens when two separate transactions are reading data. But what happens when one transaction reads data while a second is writing new data?

CONSISTENT READS

The Oracle Server makes sure that data returned from a query is consistent with respect to a moment in time. In other words, the result set must be a true snapshot of the data that has been committed when the query begins, so that modifications made after the query started do not appear in the result set.

Before discussing how the Oracle Server guarantees a consistent result set, let's take a look at the problem more closely. Suppose that at 1:20 pm, you issue the following statement:

```
SQL> SELECT emp_id, last_name, salary
  2  FROM org;
```

ORG is a large table, so your statement takes several minutes to finish executing. While the Server is scanning the table, another user issues the following statements:

```
SQL> UPDATE org
  2   SET salary = salary + 2000
  3   WHERE emp_id = 27915;


SQL> COMMIT;
```

At 1:21, before your query has finished executing, a third user issues yet another statement affecting ORG:

```
SQL> INSERT INTO org
  2   VALUES 28732, 'Wu', 'Sally', 42000;
```

At 1:22, your query has finished executing. What will be the result set? Will it include the data for Sally Wu? If it did, then your query will have performed a *dirty read*, whereby the result set includes modified but uncommitted data. The Oracle Server does not allow dirty reads.

What about the new salary for employee number 27915? This bit of data, though it is committed, also does not belong in the result set because it is inconsistent with other data produced by the query. Other salaries reflected the state of the database at 1:20, while this employee's salary reflects the database at 1:21. Therefore, this new data also should not appear in the result set.

The Oracle Server makes sure that the new data doesn't appear because it guarantees consistent reads: a SELECT statement sees no other transactions—committed or uncommitted—that occur after the SELECT statement began.

How does the Server guarantee that? We have already said that it does not lock rows accessed by a SELECT statement. Doing so would greatly reduce concurrency because it would not be enough to lock a row as it's being read: you would have to lock all rows to prevent modifications that might occur before you read a row. Clearly, locking is not the answer to read consistency.

THE MULTI-VERSION CONSISTENCY MODEL

Instead, the Oracle Server guarantees consistency by using the *multi-version consistency model*. With this model, the Server stores several versions of the same data, each version corresponding to a point in time. Users who issue queries see the version that was current when they issued the query. (Figure 6.3) Writers, meanwhile, can make modifications and store them as new versions.

Here is how this works in practice.

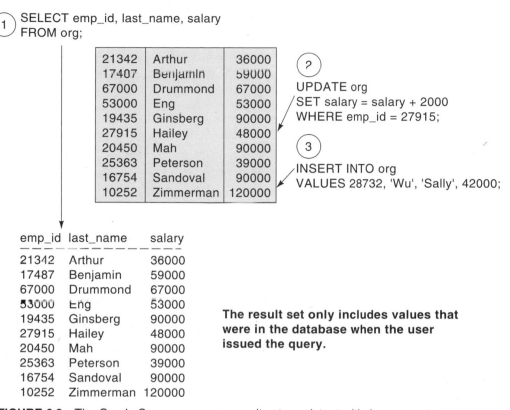

FIGURE 6.3   The Oracle Server ensures a result set consistent with the moment a query begins.

Whenever a transaction occurs, the Server assigns the transaction a *System Change Number (SCN)*. Because more recent transactions have a higher SCN, the SCN serves as a relative timestamp. When a user issues a query and this query enters execution stage, the Server notes the current SCN; it then returns only values corresponding to the SCN. Meanwhile, other transactions may modify data, but when they do, the previous values (along with their SCNs) get stored in rollback segments. That way, the Server can continue fetching values that correspond to the SCN noted when the query began. If a row has been modified since that point, the Server gets the data from the rollback segment. (Figure 6.4)

Because this model allows modifications to occur without interfering with read operations, it guarantees consistency while maintaining high concurrency.

TRANSACTION-LEVEL READ CONSISTENCY

We have seen how the Oracle Server produces a result set consistent with the start of a SELECT statement. Sometimes, though, you may want the results

```
SELECT emp_id, last_name, salary          (SCN = 200)
FROM org;
```

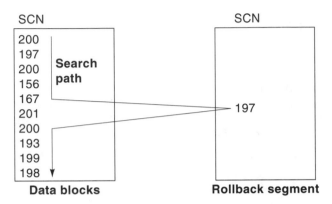

FIGURE 6.4 The Server uses rollback segments and
the SCN to find a result set consistent with a point in time.

of several statements to be consistent for a single point in time. For example, suppose you are generating a report based on several tables: the first statement queries table A, and the second statement queries table B. You want to make sure that the results of both queries represent the state of the database at the start of the first query.

Read-Only Transactions

If your transaction contains only SELECT statements, you can specify that your transaction is read-only. To do so, execute the following command before entering either query:

```
SQL> SET TRANSACTION READ ONLY;
```

Thereafter, all statements will return only data that was committed before the start of the transaction. That way, other users can modify either table at any time during the transaction without damaging the consistency of the data from one read to the next.

The following short script is an example of such a transaction:

```
SET TRANSACTION READ ONLY;
SELECT part_id, qty FROM stock
      WHERE qty < 10 AND warehouse = 'Camden';
SELECT part_id, qty FROM stock
      WHERE qty < 10 AND warehouse = 'Newark';
COMMIT;
```

This transaction will return data about both warehouses based on the time the first statement executes.

Read/Write Transactions

In some cases, your transaction will contain both SELECT statements and DML commands that modify data. Because of this combination, the SET TRANSACTION READ ONLY command will not work. The only way to ensure consistency from one read to the next in this sort of transaction is to lock the table that you don't want modified.

The following script is an example of a read/write transaction:

```
LOCK TABLE stock IN EXCLUSIVE MODE;
SELECT part_id, qty FROM stock
     WHERE qty < 10 AND warehouse = 'Camden';
UPDATE org
     SET last_name = 'Dickinson'
     WHERE emp_id = 53004;
SELECT part_id, qty FROM stock
     WIIERE qly < 10 ANU warehouse = 'Newark';
COMMIT;
```

Even though the purpose of the UPDATE statement in this transaction may not be apparent, this script does make clear the need to lock the STOCK table. The UPDATE statement does not modify STOCK, but statements from other concurrent transactions might. The LOCK TABLE command makes certain that they don't, so that the result set of this transaction is the same as the one for the same transaction without the UPDATE.

PUTTING IT ALL TOGETHER

You can now see how the Oracle Server makes sure that a query does not pick up modifications made by transactions that started after the query began. You have also learned how to ensure such read consistency for entire transactions, not just individual statements. In addition, you saw that the Server prevents one transaction from overwriting the work of another by locking rows that are being modified. Thus, the Oracle Server makes data accessible to many concurrent users while preserving the accuracy of this data, both as it's stored and as it appears to users issuing queries.

STARTING AND STOPPING AN INSTANCE

CHAPTER OVERVIEW

When users access an Oracle database, the Oracle Server must be running in order to manage all of the tasks discussed in this book. This chapter describes how to start an instance of the Server and how to bring it down when necessary for upgrade, cold (offline) backup, and other reasons.

STARTING AN INSTANCE

Though the Oracle Server is an executable program like any other, starting it requires a special utility. The reason? The Oracle Server is a complex product with many options; to specify these options and perform other administration tasks, Oracle Corporation provides special utilities.

SQL*DBA: LINE MODE VERSUS SCREEN MODE

One utility that Oracle produces for this purpose is SQL*DBA. You can use this utility in either screen mode or line mode. Screen mode, with its menus and dialog boxes, is good for users who don't know the exact syntax of the command they want to execute. For example, new users might feel more comfortable with screen mode. But even experienced DBAs performing non-routine administration tasks may want to use screen mode because it reminds them of their options. DBAs performing routine tasks such as startup and shutdown, on the other hand, generally prefer using SQL*DBA in line mode because this mode is faster if you know the exact command. In fact, experienced DBAs frequently embed SQL*DBA commands within shell scripts that perform related tasks in a predefined order.

SQL*DBA and Server Manager

Using SQL*DBA, DBAs can do much more than start and stop an instance. They can perform other administrative tasks, such as creating and backing up a database, managing security, and monitoring performance. In addition, SQL*DBA can be used to issue ordinary SQL statements.

Oracle Server Manager is a newer product, performing similar tasks but featuring a graphical user interface. It comes with versions 7.1 and higher of the Oracle Server.

INSTANCE STARTUP OPTIONS

Both modes have a command for starting an instance. Before you can start using a database, an instance must not only be started but the database itself must be mounted to the instance and open. Therefore, the default options for starting an instance include mounting and opening the default database. (Figure 7.1)

Sometimes, though, you may need to start an instance without opening, or even mounting, a database.

Mounting but Not Opening

If a data file has gotten lost or corrupted, it's impossible to open the database. The Oracle Server can recover lost data using redo information, but if you want it to do that, you must start an instance without opening the database. Other situations that require a database to be mounted but closed include adding or deleting redo log files, renaming data files or redo log files, and altering the status of archiving (ARCHIVELOG to NOARCHIVELOG or the reverse).

Once you perform the task that requires mounting but not opening a database, you do not have to shut down the instance and restart it normally. Instead, you can simply choose to open the database. SQL*DBA knows which database to open because it is already mounted to the instance.

Not Mounting or Opening

Mounting a database makes the Server read the control file (the location of which is specified in the initialization file). It reads the control file to make sure that

Starting but not mounting

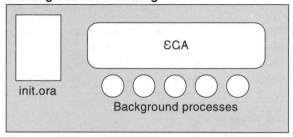

Starting and mounting, but not opening

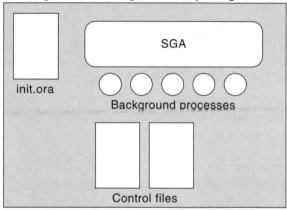

Starting, mounting, and opening

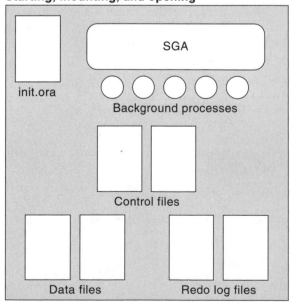

FIGURE 7.1 The three types of instance startup.

the data files and redo log files it refers to reside where the control files says they do. This step paves the way for the possible next step, which is opening the database.

If, however, the control file does not exist for some reason, the Server cannot mount the database. In such cases, the only way to proceed is to start an instance without mounting a database. Once the instance is started, you can try restoring or recreating the control file or creating a new database and then mounting and opening the database.

Mounting and Opening

Again, these situations involving missing control files or data files are rare. In most cases, you start an instance by mounting and opening a database. This close association between starting an instance and opening data files could be why many people talk about "starting up a database," rather than starting an instance.

HOW DO YOU START AN INSTANCE?

If you are using SQL*DBA in screen mode, start an instance using the Startup Instance command. This command brings up a dialog box in which you can specify the following options:

❏ whether another instance should be allowed to mount the same database (that is, whether to allow the Parallel Server to function)

❏ the name of the database to be mounted (in case you have more than one database on the machine that is running the Oracle Server)

❏ the name of the initialization parameter file to be used (in case you have multiple databases with different initialization files or if you are tuning the Server's performance by experimenting with different initialization parameters for the same database)

If you want to accept the defaults, you can bypass the dialog box by simply pressing [Return] when it appears. If you know what the defaults are and plan to accept them, it's a good idea to use SQL*DBA in line mode.

In line mode, enter the following command to start an instance and open a database called MYDATA:

```
SQLDBA> STARTUP OPEN mydata;
```

To mount the database without opening it, enter the following command instead:

```
SQLDBA> STARTUP MOUNT mydata;
```

If you simply want to start an instance without opening or even mounting a database, then enter the following command:

```
SQLDBA> STARTUP NOMOUNT;
```

All three commands shown above start an instance using the default initialization parameter file. If you want to specify a different file in SQL*DBA line mode, you must specify it following the PFILE option. For example, the following command starts an instance using the parameters specified in INITRECO.ORA:

```
SQLDBA> STARTUP MOUNT mydata PFILE=initreco.ora;
```

WHAT HAPPENS DURING INSTANCE STARTUP?

During instance startup, the Oracle Server reads the initialization parameter file you have specified using SQL*DBA. Then, using the values in that parameter file, the Server allocates enough memory for the SGA (and, in the case of UNIX operating systems, enough semaphores) and starts the background processes. In addition, if you have specified that you want to mount and open a database, the Server opens the control file, data files, and redo log files for the database.

Note that in the dedicated server configuration, the server processes—those working on behalf of the users—don't start during instance startup. This makes sense, of course, because there can be many users per instance, and having processes alive without users needing them wastes system resources, potentially degrading the Server's performance for those users that are using it. Therefore, a server process only starts when the Server receives a connection request from a user, such as when a user starts up an application that uses the Server.

SETTING INITIALIZATION PARAMETERS

There are hundreds of parameters that a DBA can set to control how an instance behaves at startup. The following list describes only some of the parameters related to topics discussed in this book.

Keep in mind that editing the initialization parameter file is optional, though highly recommended. Default values for all critical parameters are already specified in the sample file that ships with the Oracle7 Server. These will work with a small database. If your database is larger than the sample, or if for some other reason you want to use values that are different from the default values, you will need to edit the file accordingly.

DB_NAME

This parameter specifies the name of the database to be opened when the instance starts. Define this parameter before creating the database. That way, when you issue the CREATE DATABASE statement, the Server will put this name on all the database's files.

This name can be up to 8 characters long.

DB_DOMAIN

This parameter, in conjunction with DB_NAME, uniquely identifies your database among all other databases.

The value of this parameter can be up to 128 characters long, including the periods that separate its components. For example, the DB_NAME might be FINANCE, but the DB_DOMAIN could be GREATCO.US.COM. Similarly, Greatco's German office could have a database called FINANCE with a DB_DOMAIN of GREATCO.GERMANY.COM, to distinguish it from the U.S. database.

CONTROL_FILES

The value of this parameter specifies the full pathname of one or more control files for your database. Define this parameter before creating the database. That way, when you do issue the CREATE DATABASE statement, the Server creates files with the names you specified and puts them in the locations you specified.

DB_BLOCK_BUFFERS

This parameter lets you specify how many data block buffers the SGA should contain in its database buffer cache. The higher the value, the more likely it is that a user querying the database can get the result set from the cache, without having to read from disk. Therefore, higher values for DB_BLOCK_BUFFERS generally mean better performance. The cost, however, is that these buffers take away memory from other needs.

SHARED_POOL_SIZE

The value of this parameter specifies the size, in bytes, of the shared pool. As with DB_BLOCK_BUFFERS, the greater this value, the better the performance. If the value is high, then chances are that the Server can execute a SQL statement or PL/SQL block immediately since a parsed representation likely exists in the shared pool. If the shared pool is small, however, then users are likely to experience delays due to reparsing.

PROCESSES

This parameter sets the maximum number of processes that can connect to this instance at the same time. This number includes both background processes and user processes. Therefore, if you want to limit the number of concurrent users to 10, you need to set PROCESSES to 15 or 16 (depending on which background processes will be running).

CHECKPOINT_PROCESS

The value of this parameter determines whether to enable the checkpoint process (CKPT) or whether its work should be performed by LGWR. To enable CKPT, you must set this parameter to TRUE.

LOG_ARCHIVE_START

The value of this parameter determines whether the Server should automatically archive filled redo log files. Since the Server runs in NOARCHIVELOG mode by default, you must set LOG_ARCHIVE_START to TRUE if you want to enable archiving from the start. Also, you will want to set LOG_ARCHIVE_DEST to specify the destination directory for the archive files.

Besides setting these parameters, you must use a SQL statement to enable archiving. LOG_ARCHIVE_START merely specifies that if archiving is enabled, then the Server should archive filled redo logs automatically. Even if LOG_ARCHIVE_START is set to true, archiving will not begin unless you issue the following command:

```
SQLDBA> ALTER DATABASE ARCHIVELOG;
```

MTS_DISPATCHERS

Setting this parameter enables the multi-threaded server configuration. By default, the value is null, creating a dedicated server configuration.

You can have several entries for this parameter, one for each network protocol used to connect to server processes. For example, if you want to have one dispatcher for users connecting through SQL*Net TCP/IP and one for users connecting through SQL*Net AppleTalk, you would include the following entries:

```
MTS_DISPATCHERS = "TCPIP, 1"


MTS_DISPATCHERS = "ATK, 1"
```

Note that the strings for the protocols are arbitrary. The Server knows what they mean only through an entry you made for another initialization parameter, MTS_LISTENER_ADDRESS.

MTS_LISTENER_ADDRESS and MTS_DISPATCHERS are just two of the parameters used to configure a multi-threaded server.

Whenever you change a parameter requiring a system resource, make sure your system has enough resources to accommodate the value. For example, the value of DB_BLOCK_BUFFERS times the value of DB_BLOCK_SIZE cannot exceed the total memory available on your computer. This example may seem obvious, but other operating-system values may be harder to check and may require the help of your system administrator. For example, you may need to consult with your UNIX system administrator about setting the PROCESSES parameter, to make sure that the machine running the Oracle Server has enough semaphores to run with whatever value you specify.

STOPPING AN INSTANCE

Knowing how to start an instance is important, but equally important is knowing how to stop it if the situation calls for it.

WHEN DO YOU NEED TO STOP AN INSTANCE?

We have said that you need to start an instance each time you want to make a database available to users. But once an instance is started, why would you ever want to stop it?

The reasons for stopping an instance can be divided into several categories, as discussed below.

Upgrades

When upgrading the operating system, you obviously need to stop any instances that are running. You also need to stop an instance if you are upgrading the Oracle Server or other products that use the Server.

Performance Tuning

Whenever you modify the initialization parameter file, you need to restart the instance for the new file to be read.

System Maintenance

This includes such tasks as adding disks for database storage. It does not include maintenance of logical structures. In other words, adding tables and tablespaces does not require instance shutdown. On the contrary, you cannot manipulate logical structures if the Server is not running.

Data Recovery

You must perform data recovery in the case of a media failure or a power outage. Before you can do so, you must stop the current instance (if it has not died) to proceed with recovery.

HOW DO YOU STOP AN INSTANCE?

Stopping an instance is easier than starting one. As with starting up, you use SQL*DBA to stop an instance.

Normal Shutdown

Also as with startup, you have options for how to shut down an instance. The default (Normal) is best for most situations:

```
SQLDBA> SHUTDOWN NORMAL;
```

If SQL*DBA is running in screen mode, you can initiate normal shutdown by choosing Shutdown with the Normal option from the Instance menu.

During normal shutdown, the Server waits for all users to disconnect before shutting down the instance. As a result, normal shutdown can take a while to begin, depending on how long it takes for all users to disconnect. In fact, when you have many users, chances are that some will not disconnect, expecting you to kill their connections when you really need to. In such cases, you need to do just that by using immediate shutdown.

Immediate Shutdown

If you cannot wait for users to disconnect, use immediate shutdown:

```
SQLDBA> SHUTDOWN IMMEDIATE;
```

Immediate Shutdown rolls back any uncommitted transactions from the killed user sessions; it also does not wait for the database buffer cache to be written to disk. Therefore, to bring the database to a consistent state, you must briefly restart the instance so that recovery can take place. (To prevent users from connecting to this temporary instance, open the database in restricted mode.)

Then, after the Server has performed recovery, use normal shutdown:

```
SQLDBA> SHUTDOWN NORMAL;
```

This time, Normal Shutdown will begin very quickly because no users are connected and hence the Server does not have to wait for anyone to disconnect.

When you shut down an instance, you often have to shut down other processes associated with the instance. If Oracle applications are accessing a database, then an immediate shutdown of the instance will result in an abortive shutdown of application processes. Therefore, if you want a clean shutdown, it's a good idea to warn users to stop their work. Then, quit the applications, stop the SQL*Net processes, and shut down the instance.

WHAT HAPPENS DURING SHUTDOWN?

During normal shutdown, the Server waits for all users to disconnect before shutting down the instance. Then, after all users have disconnected, the Server clears the SGA by writing buffered data to data files and redo log files and by flushing the contents of the shared pool. Next, the Server closes the files, dismounts the database, and deallocates the SGA. Finally, it shuts down the background processes.

Instance shutdown makes memory available for the use of other programs.

MANAGING
SPACE USAGE

CHAPTER OVERVIEW

One of the jobs of the database administrator is to make optimal use of available disk space. This means not only fitting as much data on the available disk space as possible, but, more importantly, figuring out how to distribute the data in the most logical way to improve performance and facilitate recovery.

This chapter describes the ways the Oracle Server helps DBAs solve these space management problems.

PLANNING INITIAL SPACE USAGE

While the Server provides some flexibility in making changes later, the best time to determine space allocation is before database creation.

PLANNING FOR FAULT TOLERANCE

An important principle of allocating space to various database objects is to provide for media failures by duplicating critical data on separate physical storage devices. Creating multiple copies of the same files, while recommended, is optional.

Mirrored Control Files

To create identical copies of the control file on different disks, specify both files in the initialization parameter file for your database:

```
CONTROL_FILES = '/disk1/db/pr_control.ctl',
                '/disk2/db/pr_control.ctl'
```

These two files are exactly the same in name and content, but one resides on disk1 while the other resides on disk2. If one of the disks crashes, the other will contain this important file.

Mirrored Redo Log Files

The same principle applies to the redo log files. The difference is that every Oracle database consists of at least two different redo log files. Therefore, to provide one level of mirroring, you must specify at least four redo log files. You do this by using the CREATE DATABASE command to place identical redo log files in a group, with one group for each unique file:

```
SQLDBA> CREATE DATABASE pubrel
            LOGFILE GROUP 1 ('/disk1/data/pr_log1.log',
                    '/disk2/data/pr_log1.log') SIZE 30K,
                GROUP 2 ('/disk1/data/pr_log2.log',
                    '/disk2/data/pr_log2.log') SIZE 30K,

            .
            . ;
```

As a result of this command, the loss of one disk would cause the loss of just one member in each group. The other member, containing identical information, would serve as the backup.

SETTING UP TABLESPACES

When you create a database, the first data files are automatically allocated in the SYSTEM tablespace. This makes sense because as soon as you start creating tables, users, and other schema objects for your new database, the Server needs to store information about them in the data dictionary, which corresponds to the SYSTEM tablespace.

But while it makes sense for these initial data dictionary files to go into the SYSTEM tablespace, it is generally better to store user files—those containing data accessed by users—in another tablespace. This separation reduces contention (between users accessing schema objects and the Server and DBAs accessing the data dictionary) for the same data files. Keeping user-needed data out of the SYSTEM tablespace also gives the DBA the flexibility to work with the USERS tablespace without affecting the SYSTEM tablespace. In fact, some tasks that you can do with an ordinary tablespace—such as taking it offline—cannot be done to the SYSTEM tablespace at all. For these reasons, it is a good idea after creating the initial database (with its SYSTEM tablespace) to create at least one other tablespace:

```
SQLDBA> CREATE TABLESPACE users
              DATAFILE '/usr/users/datafile1.dbf' SIZE 15M;
```

Notice that this command simultaneously creates a datafile and a tablespace to which that data file should belong.

A USERS tablespace to supplement the SYSTEM tablespace may be enough for a small database, but for larger databases, you might want to create several tablespaces in place of USERS. For example, you might create a separate tablespace for storing index segments, another one for rollback segments, and a third for data segments.

Then, after creating your tablespaces, you can begin creating clusters, tables, indexes, and rollback segments in those tablespaces. You don't have to specify the tablespace for objects that you create: depending on what user account creates the objects, the objects will go into the user's default tablespace, as assigned by the DBA. But while specifying a tablespace during object creation is optional, it's a good idea to organize the objects in logical groups by explicitly assigning them a tablespace.

For example, to create a table in the USERS tablespace, issue the following command:

```
SQLDBA> CREATE TABLE students
              (student_id NUMBER(8)    PRIMARY KEY,
              last_name   VARCHAR2(15),
              .
              .)
              TABLESPACE users;
```

To create a rollback segment in the RB_SEGS tablespace, issue the following command:

```
SQLDBA> CREATE PUBLIC ROLLBACK SEGMENT rollbck_rbk
              TABLESPACE rb_segs;
```

SETTING THE SIZE OF DATA FILES

To minimize data fragmentation, the Oracle7 Server allocates space for data files when you create a database. If the Server did not preallocate space, and simply took disk space on an as-needed basis, it could not guarantee that related data—such as data used by a single application—would be stored contiguously. (Figure 8.1)

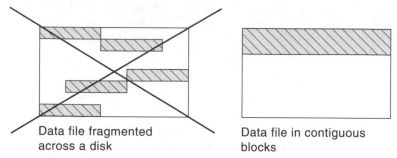

Data file fragmented across a disk

Data file in contiguous blocks

FIGURE 8.1 The Server places related data in contiguous sections.

In order for the Server to allocate space for a data file, you must tell it how much to allocate, using the CREATE DATABASE command. For example, to create a PUBREL database with an initial data file of 20 Mb, you would enter a command containing the following lines:

```
SQLDBA> CREATE DATABASE pubrel
           .
           .
        DATAFILE '/usr/pr/datafile1.dbf' SIZE 20M;
```

What Happens When You Create a Datafile that Already Exists?

When you create a database and specify a data file for it, the Server creates a file with that name. Consequently, if a file with that name already exists, it gets overwritten.

This behavior, which may seem undesirable, is not unique to the Oracle Server. The Server merely follows the lead of most operating systems, which assume that when you create a file, you truly want a new file. Like UNIX systems, the Server simply follows your instructions, not warning you that a file of that name already exists.

Therefore, it is your responsibility not to overwrite files that you need. Using unique, meaningful file names (rather than accepting the default names) is one safeguard. Another is to specify fully all files, so as to reduce the likelihood that the Server will put a file in a directory containing another file of the same name. Overall, your best strategy is to keep a record of the files, tablespaces, and schema objects that you create. This record will serve you well when you decide to alter or drop any objects.

Correctly setting the size of each data file using the CREATE DATABASE command is important because you may not be able to change it later. In Version 7.2 of the Oracle Server, you will be able to use ALTER DATABASE...RESIZE, but if you use this command to make the data file larger, then you cannot control the location of the new segment. When you initially set the size using CREATE DATABASE, in contrast, all segments will be contiguous if you start with a clean disk.

How do you determine how large to make your data files? As you might guess, the size depends on how much data your database will store. Once you know that, determine how many files you want to keep the data in, so that you know how large each file should be.

In general, it is better to create only a few large files (as opposed to many small files). There are several reasons for this. First, your operating system may impose a limit on the number of files that can be open at any one time. Also, when you create a large file, the file fills up more slowly, which means that you will not have to add more files as frequently—if at all.

SETTING THE SIZE OF DATABASE BLOCKS

Another issue to consider when creating a database is the size of each database block. By default, the operating system running the Oracle Server determines the size of each database block. You can alter this size by setting the initialization parameter DB_BLOCK_SIZE. If you want this block size to be in effect for the database you are creating, you must set it in the initialization file before starting the instance in which you are creating the database.

In general, the larger each block, the fewer reads from disk are necessary to fetch data. However, if you only want to update one row in a block, then having a large block means reading in more data than necessary.

ALTERING SPACE USAGE

As your database grows and changes, you might need to allocate more disk space to it. This section explains the options available to you for determining where new data is stored.

ADDING TABLESPACES

We have already said that a new database requires one or more new tablespaces. But even when you are merely adding tables or indexes to an existing database, a new tablespace might be in order if the new objects are logically different from existing objects. For example, if you are installing a new Oracle product that requires the creation of many tables—tables unrelated to your current tables—you may not want that data using the same tablespace as existing data.

Ways to Add Tablespaces

Adding more tablespaces is no different from other administrative tasks in that you can do it in one of several ways. Earlier in this chapter, you saw how you can use SQL*DBA in line mode to issue the CREATE TABLESPACE command, specifying which data files to create for that new tablespace. Alternatively, you can use SQL*DBA in screen mode. If you have access to Server Manager, you might prefer to use that utility.

How the Server Knows Which Database
the New Tablespaces and Data Files Belong To

You might wonder how the Server associates the new tablespace and its data files with a particular database. After all, the command for creating a tablespace only specifies which data files to create. Since the data files have not been previously created as part of CREATE DATABASE, how does the Server know which database the files are part of?

The Server knows because you can only create or alter tablespaces when an instance is running and a database is mounted and open. Recall that an instance can only be mounted to a single database. Therefore, any DDL commands you execute in that instance affect that one database. When you execute a DDL command that affects the physical structure of the database, the Server notes the changes in that database's data dictionary and in the control file. For example, when you add a tablespace, you create one or more data files; the Server then stores the name of the new tablespace in the data dictionary of the database that is open, and it stores the names of the new data files in this database's control file.

ADDING DATA FILES

Another option for increasing the capacity of your database is to add data files. (Figure 8.2) Remember that a tablespace stores logically related data. Therefore, if your database is merely growing in size—not in complexity—it is probably best to add data files to existing tablespaces.

If you are using SQL*DBA in screen mode, choose the Tablespace > Add Data File option from the Storage menu. Then, from the dialog box that appears, select one of the existing tablespaces and type the name of the data file you want to add.

If you are using SQL*DBA in line mode, simply enter a command like the following:

```
SQLDBA> ALTER TABLESPACE users
             ADD DATAFILE '/usr/users/datafile4.dbf' SIZE 15M;
```

REMOVING TABLESPACES

At times, you will find that you are storing data that is no longer being used. Ever on the lookout for ways to gain extra disk space, you decide to delete the data from hard disk after creating a full backup copy on CD-ROM, just in case.

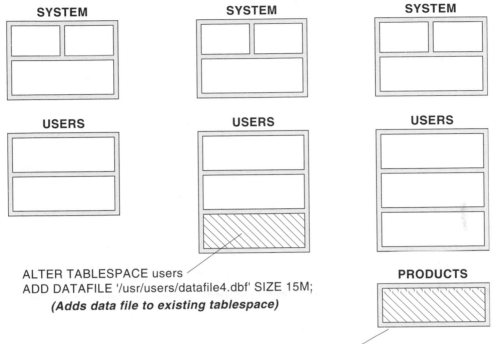

ALTER TABLESPACE users
ADD DATAFILE '/usr/users/datafile4.dbf' SIZE 15M;
(Adds data file to existing tablespace)

CREATE TABLESPACE products
DATAFILE '/usr/products/datafile1.dbf' SIZE 15M;
(Creates new tablespace with new data file)

FIGURE 8.2   Creating a new tablespace versus adding a data file to an existing tablespace.

How do you implement your plan using the Oracle Server? If you did a good job of planning your database originally, your task now is simple because all the data you want to delete should already be concentrated in one or more dedicated tablespaces.

To remove these unneeded tablespaces, choose Tablespace > Drop from the Storage menu in SQL*DBA. From the dialog box that appears, choose the tablespace you want to drop. If you want to drop any tables or other objects that are still in the tablespace, select the Drop Contained Objects, If Present option. The line-mode equivalent of this command is:

```
SQLDBA> DROP TABLESPACE 1982data INCLUDING CONTENTS;
```

DELETING DATA FILES

Dropping a tablespace and its logical contents does not delete the data files. To reclaim disk space taken up by those files, you must delete the files using an operating-system utility such as **rm** in UNIX. You must be extremely careful to delete only those files that belong to the tablespace you dropped.

To find out which data files belong to the tablespace you dropped, query the data dictionary view DBA_DATA_FILES:

```
SQLDBA> SELECT file_name
            FROM sys.dba_data_files
            WHERE tablespace_name = '1982data';
```

You must issue this query before dropping the tablespace. Then, delete only the files in the result set.

Documentation you will receive from Oracle Corporation when you order the Oracle Server contains detailed information about DBA_DATA_FILES and other useful data dictionary views.

FURTHER CONTROLLING SPACE USAGE

This section describes more techniques that DBAs can use to control how data is stored in an Oracle7 database.

CONTROLLING BLOCK USAGE

You can control space usage at the block level by using two parameters to some CREATE and ALTER commands. When you create or alter a table, cluster, or index, you can use the parameter PCTFREE. When you create or alter a table or cluster, you can use the parameter PCTUSED, as well.

PCTFREE

The value of this parameter ("percent free") tells the Server what percentage of a block to keep free for changes to rows in the block. When you create a new table and set PCTFREE to 20, for example, you tell the Server to leave 20 percent of the block for changes to rows in that block.

The purpose of PCTFREE is to minimize disk I/O. To understand how PCT-FREE minimizes disk I/O, consider what would happen without PCTFREE, which is equivalent to PCTFREE being set to 0. Suppose that a newly-created row takes up 70 percent of a block—call it Block A. When another row is created, that second row also gets stored in Block A. Now Block A is 100 percent full. If a user updates the first row, this additional information cannot fit in Block A. Therefore, the Server moves the first row to Block B, which has room for the row's new value. The Server stores Block B's address in Block A, chaining the row across the two blocks. As a result, a statement that selects this row requires two reads—one from A and one from B—instead of one.

Row Migration and Row Chaining

The purpose of using PCTFREE is to reduce row chaining and row migration, both of which involve moving row data—in part or in whole—from one data block to another.

When a user updates a row, sometimes the new values do not fit in the original data block. This happens when a user changes the value of a variable-length field to a longer value than it had before or when the user specifies a value for a field that was previously NULL. When this happens, the Server moves the whole row to another block, if the row fits completely into the second block. The original data block stores the new address—a forwarding address, in effect—so that an index generated on the table can still find the rows. This movement of an entire row to a new block is called *row migration*.

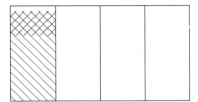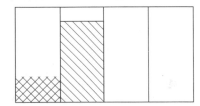

Update of row ⧅ makes the row larger than the free space in the first block, causing it to migrate to another block.

FIGURE 8.3   Row migration.

If, on the other hand, the whole row cannot fit in either the original block or the new data block as a result of the update, the Server has no choice but to move only part of it. This splitting of a row across multiple blocks is called *row chaining*.

This chaining of a row from one block to another has a cost. A query requiring a read from disk takes one I/O to read the original data block and another I/O for the new block that stores the row. This extra I/O slows down the execution of the query. Row migration has the same effect because it, too, requires a read from the original data block before reading the block that stores the row.

(Continued on next page)

Row Migration and Row Chaining (Continued)

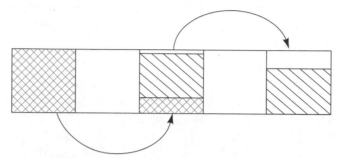

Row ▨▨ is chained from the start. The other
row gets chained as a result of an update.

FIGURE 8.4   Row chaining.

PCTFREE prevents chaining and migration, and thus improves performance, by reserving space in the original block for updates. But PCTFREE
cannot prevent chaining entirely. If a row is too large to fit in one block from
the start, then it will be stored as a chain on insert. This usually happens if
the row contains a field of datatype LONG or LONG RAW. Obviously,
PCTFREE cannot prevent row chaining in this situation.

If, in contrast, PCTFREE had been set to 20 when this table was created, then
the second row to be inserted would not fit in Block A. Therefore it would go into
Block B, leaving room in both blocks for future updates. If an update did not
increase the size of the row by more than 20 percent, then row chaining would not
occur and reads from disk could be performed with fewer I/O operations.

Another use of the space set aside by PCTFREE is to store transaction entries,
but only if the preallocated space for such entries is not enough for the number of
transactions concurrently accessing the block. In other words, if more transactions
are accessing a particular block than the block header can fit data for, some of this
transaction data will be stored in the block's free space.

PCTUSED

The value of this parameter ("percent used") tells the Server what percentage
of a block it must fill with new rows before going to a new block to insert the row.
When the percentage of a data block that is used falls down to the value of
PCTUSED, the block becomes available for inserts.

Free Lists

Each table has associated with it lists of data blocks that have been allocated for that table. These lists contain free space for inserting rows, and, consequently, are called *free lists*. Items on the free list are those data blocks that are less full than PCTUSED. For example, if a block's PCTUSED parameter is 60 and the block is only 40 percent full, the block belongs on the free list.

When a user issues an INSERT, the Server tries to insert the record (row) into the block that is at the top of the free list. If the whole record fits into the space left in the block's PCTUSED space, then the Server inserts the record into that block. If not, it tries inserting the record into the next block on the free list.

As deletes and updates make more or less space available, blocks move on and off the free list.

To see how the Server uses PCTUSED to decide which blocks should remain available for inserts, consider a table defined with PCTFREE as 20 and PCTUSED as 60:

a. If the block is 80 percent full, it is not on the free list because the remaining 20 percent is reserved for updates to existing rows. (Figure 8.5a)

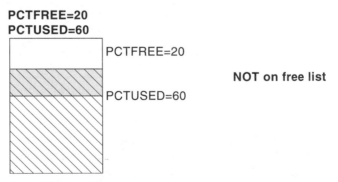

FIGURE 8.5a If the block is 80 percent full, it is not on the free list because the remaining 20 percent is reserved for updates to existing rows.

b. Even if a delete or update brings the percentage full to a number between PCTFREE and PCTUSED (such as 68 percent), the block stays off the free list. (Figure 8.5b)

FIGURE 8.5b Even if a delete or update brings the percentage full to a number between PCTFREE and PCTUSED (such as 68 percent), the block stays off the free list.

c. If a delete or update causes the block to be less full than PCTUSED (such as 57 percent), the block moves back onto the free list. (Figure 8.5c)

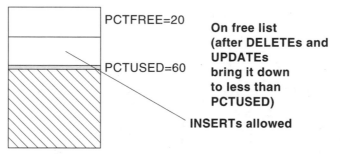

FIGURE 8.5c If a delete or update causes the block to be less full than PCTUSED (such as 57 percent), the block moves back onto the free list.

d. and e. Once the block is on the free list, the Server continues inserting new rows into it (Figure 8-5d) until the block has no more space for new rows, only for updates (Figure 8-5e). In our example, this happens when the block becomes 80 percent full.

In all cases, (PCTUSED + PCTFREE) must be less than 100.

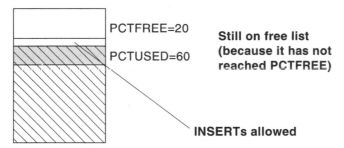

FIGURE 8.5d   Once the block is on the free list, the Server
continues inserting new rows into it.

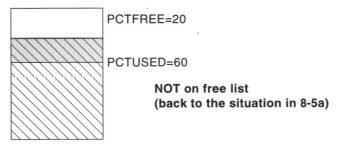

FIGURE 8.5e   The Server stops inserting rows in the block
when the block has no more space for new rows, only
for updates.

You can see that by setting PCTUSED to a high number such as 80, you make it likely that data blocks will be fuller than if you set PCTUSED to a lower number. But this efficient use of block space comes at the cost of performance. With PCTUSED set high, blocks will remain on the free list even if none of them have enough space to accommodate most inserts. Ideally, you don't want blocks to be on the free list unless they contain enough space to insert at least one row. If blocks are on the free list, the Server must continue checking them whenever a user issues an INSERT, even if there is no space to insert the row. This checking creates a bottleneck.

To avoid this bottleneck, leave some slack space between PCTFREE and PCTUSED, sizing PCTUSED based on the size of a typical row in the table. By setting PCTUSED in such a way that it and PCTFREE add up to less than 100, you make the Server use the free list more efficiently, even though it will not use up every byte of available block space.

CONTROLLING EXTENT ALLOCATION

Recall that data blocks in a table, index, or cluster are organized in contiguous sets called *extents*. The Oracle Server automatically allocates additional extents when more space is needed to store new data within the same object. For example, when a table grows and the first extent fills up, the Server allocates an additional extent for storing the extra data.

This kind of dynamic allocation, however, comes at a cost because allocating extents uses some system resources. To minimize this cost, the DBA can set extent storage parameters, telling the Server when and how to allocate extents.

INITIAL

This parameter sets the size of the first extent. For example, if you expect your table to be 50K, and you don't want the Server to allocate additional extents, set INITIAL to 50K. All the table's data will then be stored in the initial extent; while the table is growing, however, parts of the extent may go unused.

NEXT

This parameter sets the size of the next extent that the Server allocates.

PCTINCREASE

This parameter ("percent increase") sets the growth rate of subsequent extents. If set to 0, each extent after the initial extent will take on the value of NEXT. If PCTINCREASE is set to 100, then each additional extent will be twice the size of the previous extent.

MINEXTENTS

This parameter tells the Server how many extents to allocate during object creation. For example, if you give MINEXTENTS the value 3, INITIAL the value 50, NEXT the value 50, and you omit the PCTINCREASE parameter, the Server will create a table with 3 extents of 50K each. As the table grows, it may allocate additional extents if the value of MAXEXTENTS is higher than 3.

Since this parameter dictates what happens during object creation, you can only specify it once, using the CREATE command. It makes no sense to use it with the ALTER command.

MAXEXTENTS

This parameter determines the maximum number of extents that can be allocated for the object; it thus sets a cap on the size of the object. For example, if you create a table with INITIAL and NEXT of 100K, PCTINCREASE of 0, and MAXEXTENTS of 4, then, at most, your table can take up 400K. If you realize later that you underestimated the table's space needs, you can change the value of MAXEXTENTS by using the ALTER TABLE command.

These parameters can be specified as part of the STORAGE clause of certain CREATE and ALTER commands. Or, you can set storage values for an entire tablespace using a database administration utility, and then let the table or other object take on the storage values of the tablespace to which it belongs.

SETTING TABLESPACE QUOTAS

As a DBA, you can set limits on how much of a tablespace each user can fill with new schema objects. The idea is to allow some qualified users to create tables, views, and other such objects but to maintain central control over how these objects are stored.

You can set tablespace quotas when you create users. For each user, you can specify how much disk space the user can use for a particular tablespace. After creating a user, you can change the user's tablespace quotas. For example, to keep user DHOG from using more than 1 Mb of space in the USERS tablespace, enter the following command:

```
SQLDBA> ALTER USER dhog
          QUOTA 1M ON users;
```

You will learn more about creating users in the chapter on security.

OPTIMIZING PERFORMANCE

CHAPTER OVERVIEW

Beyond the day-to-day tasks of managing a database system, a DBA can follow special procedures to improve the performance of the system. In this chapter, when we speak about performance, we are talking about how quickly users can access data in an Oracle database.

More so than other areas covered in this book, performance tuning is a large and complex topic. It is in many ways a craft, one to which specialists devote years to mastering. This chapter provides an overview of the types of steps you can take to improve the performance of an Oracle database.

OPTIMIZING THE USE OF MEMORY

The Oracle Server relies very heavily on memory. The whole idea of the SGA is to keep as much information in memory as possible so as to reduce time-consuming reads from disk. Therefore, the most obvious way to improve the performance of the Oracle Server is to make the SGA as large as possible.

TOTAL MEMORY

Of course, the size of the SGA is limited by the amount of memory available on the machine on which the Oracle Server is run. Some operating systems offer *virtual memory*, which creates the illusion of extra memory by swapping information between main memory and disk. On such operating systems, it is possible to increase the size of the SGA by dipping into virtual memory. In practice, though, doing so actually tends to degrade the performance of the Server. Swapping involves disk I/O, the time-consuming activity that the SGA is designed to reduce. Too much movement of data between disk and memory requires more resources than it saves. To make sure that such excessive swapping does not occur, a DBA can use an operating-system utility to monitor a machine's swapping activity.

In general, though, the most effective way to improve Oracle's performance is to maximize the amount of real memory available for the SGA. This might mean dedicating a machine to the Oracle Server, so that other programs do not take away memory from the SGA. Or it might mean adding more memory to your machine.

Very Large Memory

How large is large? When you talk about an SGA, size is relative to the needs of the database users. Some Oracle customers have databases that are many gigabytes in size. Using a Digital UNIX operating system running on an Alpha system, engineers at Oracle tested the limits of the performance of the Oracle Server by allocating a 10-gigabyte SGA, an SGA large enough to store the entire contents of a large company's database. With an SGA that size, no reads from disk are necessary for accessing data. In fact, the only I/O activity consists of occasional deferred writes from the buffers to disk to secure the data and writes from the log buffer.

Such a large memory was possible only because of the Alpha chip's unique 64-bit architecture. Other computers, which use a 32-bit architecture, simply do not have enough address space for such a large memory. But as other hardware vendors adopt 64-bit technology, large in-memory databases may become commonplace.

Despite the importance of a large amount of real memory, size isn't everything. Almost as important is properly allocating whatever amount of memory you do have to the various parts of the SGA.

SGA ALLOCATION

Recall that the SGA consists of the database block buffers, the log buffer, and the shared pool. While you may not have control over the amount of memory available for the SGA, you can control how that memory is used. You do that by setting the initialization parameters DB_BLOCK_SIZE, DB_BLOCK_BUFFERS, LOG_BUFFER, and SHARED_POOL_SIZE.

In addition, if your instance is configured to use the multi-threaded server, session information gets stored in the SGA, as well. The actual amount of memory used for this purpose depends on how many user sessions are active.

In a dedicated-server configuration, though, the size of the SGA is determined by the following simple formula:

SGA = DB_BLOCK_SIZE x DB_BLOCK_BUFFERS + LOG_BUFFER + SHARED_POOL_SIZE. (Figure 9.1)

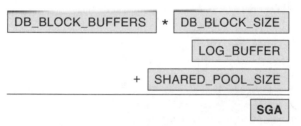

FIGURE 9.1 The size of the SGA is the sum of the values of several initialization parameters.

Gathering Performance Statistics

How can you tell how much space to allocate to one part of the equation relative to another? You do this by running an instance with some test values set, and gathering statistics about cache hits and cache misses to different memory caches.

A *cache hit* occurs when a user requests information that is already in the cache. A *cache miss* occurs when requested information is not in the cache. The *cache hit ratio* is the percentage of queries that result in a cache hit.

Then you analyze your statistics to determine how to adjust the initialization parameters. Statistics come from several dynamic performance tables. A *dynamic performance table* is a table the Server maintains and updates constantly to reflect the changing status or activity of various processes. For example, there are dynamic performance tables to track the activity of locks and of log files. Others track the performance of library, dictionary, and database buffer caches. When a DBA monitors performance using a utility like SQL*DBA, the utility selects columns from these tables to give the DBA the info that he or she needs.

Even though it is not necessary for a DBA to access these tables directly, since SQL*DBA does that work, it helps to understand what data the tables contain. Let's take a look at one dynamic performance table, V$SYSSTAT, to get an understanding of these tables in general.

V$SYSSTAT is actually a view on another table that the Server uses to keep track of buffer cache statistics. Among other data, this table stores the names of several statistics (including requests for data and physical reads) along with their corresponding current values. Since a physical read constitutes a cache miss, you can calculate the cache hit ratio by using the following formula:

Cache hit ratio = 1 − (physical reads / logical reads)

As the instance continues running, the values in each of the columns in V$SYSSTAT change, possibly changing the cache hit ratio for the database buffer cache.

Again, V$SYSSTAT is just one of several tables that yield helpful performance statistics. To determine which initialization parameters need to be raised, you will be drawing on statistics from tables that monitor other parts of the SGA. For example, V$ROWCACHE stores statistics about data dictionary cache hits, while V$LIBRARYCACHE stores similar statistics about the library cache.

Analyzing Performance Statistics

As with any gathering of statistics, it's important to get a sampling that's representative of overall activity. In the case of performance statistics, this means gathering them during different times in an instance's life cycle. For example, when you first start an instance, all the caches will be *cold* (empty) because users and applications will not have loaded them with data. Therefore, the cache hit ratios at this time will be low no matter how the SGA initialization parameters are set. It would be unwise to infer much from these initial statistics. Instead, a DBA should monitor the performance of the caches as they "heat up" and stabilize as the day progresses.

After you have gathered accurate statistics, you must interpret them to determine what action to take as a result. To make wise adjustments to the SGA parameters, you need to know which ratios are good and which ones are unacceptable. Cache misses to the shared pool, for example, are more detrimental to performance than misses to the database buffer cache. Table 9.1 gives rules of thumb for good cache hit ratios to the various caches.

TABLE 9.1

Cache	Good Cache Hit Ratio is at or above...
data dictionary	85%
library	90%
data buffer	60%

If you are getting a lower hit ratio for one of the caches, raise the corresponding initialization parameter. To allow for this adjustment, lower the value of a parameter which might be unnecessarily high. For example, consider the following situation. Suppose you set the data buffer size to 50M and the shared pool size to 20M. After letting the Server run with these settings, you find that your hit ratio to the data buffer cache was 97%, while your hit ratio to the library cache was 90%, and the hit ratio to the dictionary cache was only 70%. Seeing that the hit ratio of the data buffer cache is so high, and knowing that 70% is too low a hit ratio for the data dictionary cache, you adjust your parameter settings. You lower the value of DB_BLOCK_BUFFERS but increase the value of SHARED_POOL_SIZE, and restart the instance. After a few iterations of this process, you find parameter settings that provide optimal results.

OPTIMIZING THE USE OF DISK RESOURCES

After you have done all you can to make the best use of memory, you will likely find that you are still experiencing cache misses. In the case of a cache miss, the Server must go to disk to get the requested data. This section describes how you can make the best use of disk resources to improve performance.

REDUCING CONTENTION

Performance slows down when several processes have to use the same disk. For example, suppose the redo log files and data files are on the same disk. If the Database Writer is trying to write to a data file while the Log Writer is flushing the redo log onto the redo log file, the Database Writer must wait for the Log Writer to finish its job.

Separating Redo Log Files from Data Files

Keeping data files on a separate disk from redo log files reduces time-consuming contention for the same disk space. It also achieves another benefit: in the case of a disk failure, only one of the files will be destroyed. Just as the President and Vice-President fly in separate planes, so should your data files and redo log files be on separate disks. (Figure 9.2)

Storing the control file on the same disk as the other database files does not promote contention because the control file gets accessed so infrequently compared to the others. Nonetheless, if you have the extra disk, it's a good idea to store the control file separately (or to keep a mirrored copy on another disk) in case a problem does occur.

Separating Indexes from Their Tables

A table and an index should be on different data files, and, moreover, these data files should be on different disks.

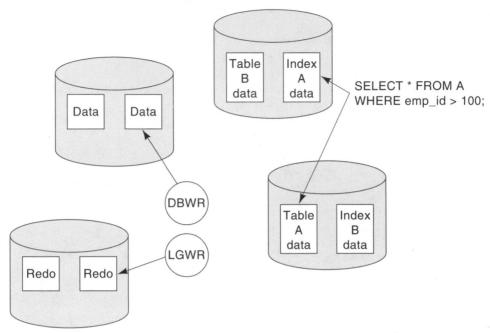

FIGURE 9.2   Reducing disk contention.

REDUCING FRAGMENTATION

While it is a good idea to keep different objects on separate disks, it is important to avoid fragmenting your data. That is, on any piece of physical storage, logically related data—such as the data in a row of a table—should be stored in contiguous blocks.

The chapter on managing space usage explains how to reduce fragmentation.

USING THE MULTI-THREADED SERVER

In some cases, you can improve the performance of the Oracle Server by configuring it to use the multi-threaded server. To understand the benefits of the mult-threaded server, it's helpful to understand its counterpart, the dedicated server.

With the dedicated server, each user process launches its own server process. If 100 users are connected to an Oracle instance, there are 100 server processes. Assuming there is enough memory available, each server process responds quickly to its user process because it is dedicated to serving it; that is, serving that user process is its entire job. In fact, while the user process is not making any requests, the server process just sits idle waiting for other requests from the same user.

If, on the other hand, the system is short on memory, the dedicated server processes are not able to process user requests quickly because system resources get taken up just keeping the server processes alive, even as the processes idle.

The multi-threaded server gets around this problem. Instead of one server process per user process, the multi-threaded server uses *shared server processes*, processes shared by user processes. One or more *dispatcher processes* field requests from user processes and send them on to available server processes. Depending on the nature of the user processes, it might make sense to use 10 shared server processes and 2 dispatcher processes instead of 100 dedicated server processes to serve 100 users.

Is Oracle Case-Sensitive?

Under any operating system, the Oracle Server understands SQL commands regardless of whether they are entered as uppercase or lowercase.

However, while such commands have the same meaning, the Server does not initially see them as identical. That is, it stores a separate copy of each version of the statement in the shared pool, so that if SELECT * FROM ORG is already in the SGA and a user enters SELECT* FROM org, the Server will have to parse and execute the statement as if it were a new statement. Therefore, for optimal performance, all SQL statements should be entered using identical case conventions. The same is true for the use of white space.

OPTIMIZING QUERIES

One of the components of the Oracle Server is a query optimizer, called simply the optimizer. Its goal is to speed up the execution of DML statements, and it does so by simplifying SQL statements and by determining execution plans.

Simplifying SQL statements means transforming what the user has entered into a slightly lower-level equivalent, one that is easier for a computer to execute. For example, if the user enters a statement with a BETWEEN operator—a valid operator in SQL—the optimizer translates the statement to one using <=, >=, and AND.

Determining an execution plan involves figuring out the best path to follow in fetching requested data and then performing the logic to limit the answer to what the user has requested. In figuring out the best execution plan, the optimizer can use one of two methods, described below.

RULE-BASED METHOD

With the rule-based method, the optimizer uses some general principles to determine the best execution plan.

The rule-based approach works by first analyzing the SQL statement to determine which access paths are possible based on two factors:

❑ the information provided in the SQL statement

❑ the existence of such objects as indexes and hash clusters, which are discussed later in this chapter, that may speed up access to data in the table being queried

Then, having narrowed down its choices to those access paths that are possible for this particular statement, the optimizer picks the highest-ranked access path for executing the statement. That's where the rules come in. The optimizer has a rule, for example, that says to access by ROWID rather than by hash cluster key. Another rule is that optimizer should access by a composite index rather than through a full table scan. In fact, the optimizer would only use a full table scan if it is the only access method available.

We can summarize how the rule-based optimizer works by saying that it follows only one rule: pick the highest-ranked access path available from a predetermined list of rankings. (Figure 9.3)

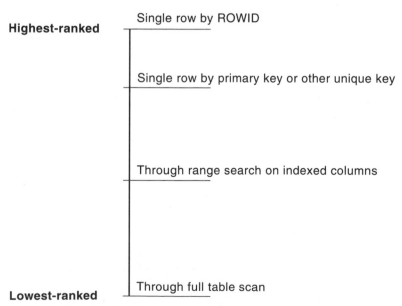

Highest-ranked   Single row by ROWID

Single row by primary key or other unique key

Through range search on indexed columns

Through full table scan

Lowest-ranked

FIGURE 9.3   The rankings of some of the access paths, from highest to lowest. The rule-based optimizer chooses the highest-ranked access path available.

Once it determines the fastest path using these heuristics, it recommends the fastest access path available.

For example, consider the following query:

```
SQL> SELECT last_name, first_name
  2  FROM org
  3  WHERE emp_id = 11460;
```

The Server can execute this query through one of several methods. Available with any query, of course, is the full table scan. But recall that EMP_ID is the primary key for ORG: only one row matches the condition in the WHERE clause. Therefore, the "single row by unique or primary key" access path is also available. Of these two available choices, the rule-based optimizer uses the latter because it is ranked higher than a full table scan.

Because the rankings for the various access paths are preset, the rule-based optimizer will always choose the same execution plan for any single SQL statement, regardless of the state of the underlying table. But because data in different tables and databases may be stored differently, the rule-based optimizer may not always determine the best plan for a particular database.

COST-BASED METHOD

If the optimizer uses the cost-based method, a feature new to Oracle7, it finds the best execution plan based on the anticipated cost of applying each plan to the specific database being accessed. While cost is a combination of I/O, memory, and other resources needed to execute the query using a particular plan, cost essentially equals time. The less time the optimizer anticipates a particular execution plan will take, the lower its cost, and the more likely the optimizer will choose that plan.

To calculate the cost of a particular plan, the optimizer analyzes statistics about the objects being accessed. For a table, these statistics include the number of rows, the average length of a row, the number of used and unused data blocks, and so forth. After comparing the costs of the various available execution plans, the optimizer tells the Server how to execute the statement by recommending the lowest-cost plan.

Where do these statistics come from? Since there are so many statistics to keep track of, and since they are constantly changing as the database changes, the Server does not keep track of all the statistics all the time. Instead, a DBA must use the ANALYZE command to explicitly tell the Server to generate the statistics for a particular schema object.

For example, to tell the Server to generate statistics for the STUDENTS table, you would enter the following command:

```
SQLDBA> ANALYZE TABLE students COMPUTE STATISTICS;
```

The resulting statistics get stored in the data dictionary and become available to the cost-based optimizer. As your database changes, the statistics become dated and therefore do not lead to optimal execution plans. To gather new statistics, you must issue the ANALYZE command again.

After you regenerate statistics, the same queries you issued before might be executed using a different access path. Because the object has changed, the relative costs of accessing it using different access methods may have changed as well. Contrast this behavior with that of the rule-based optimizer, where the same query always get carried out using the same access path, so long as the objects that make that path possible are present.

CHOOSING A METHOD

You can tell the optimizer which method to use for a given instance by setting the initialization parameter OPTIMIZER_MODE to either CHOOSE or RULE. The values may seem self-explanatory, but there's a small catch. If you specify CHOOSE and no statistics are available for executing a particular query—that is, if the ANALYZE command has not been executed for the relevant schema objects—the Server will use the rule-based optimizer for that query.

Why, then, not always specify CHOOSE? The potential problem is that if you specify CHOOSE and only some statistics are available, the optimizer will use those statistics to find a cost-based execution plan. But because the optimizer is using only limited information, this plan may not be efficient. It may actually take longer to execute than a plan found through the rule-based method. As with many aspects of performance optimization, there's a trade-off involved. In this case, the trade-off is between spending a lot of time gathering statistics to get an excellent execution plan and spending no time gathering statistics but getting a plan that's not necessarily optimal for your specific table.

If you do want to use the cost-based method but don't want to spend a lot of time generating statistics, you can tell the Server just to estimate the statistics by executing ANALYZE with the ESTIMATE option:

```
SQLDBA> ANALYZE TABLE students ESTIMATE STATISTICS;
```

Estimating, which involves gathering statistics for only a sampling of the table, is obviously faster than computing exact statistics by looking at the whole table.

You can also affect the behavior of the optimizer through the use of the ALTER SESSION parameter OPTIMIZER_GOAL. Through this parameter, you can tell the Server what you mean by "optimize." For example, if you are primarily concerned with getting the full answer as quickly as possible, you would probably choose ALL_ROWS:

```
SQLDBA> ALTER SESSION
  SET OPTIMIZER_GOAL = ALL_ROWS;
```

If, however, your goal is to improve the response time—that is, the time between when a user enters the command and when the data begins appearing—then choose FIRST_ROWS:

```
SQLDBA> ALTER SESSION
  SET OPTIMIZER_GOAL = FIRST_ROWS;
```

When you choose FIRST_ROWS, the optimizer finds the execution plan that will bring up the first responses to the query, even if it means that the rest of the results will take longer to appear.

USING INDEXES AND HASH CLUSTERS

The optimizer speeds up the performance of queries by finding the best execution plan from among those that are possible. Most efficient execution plans rely on the presence of an index or a hash cluster. Thus, by creating these objects you help the Server execute SQL statements more quickly.

INDEXES

As noted earlier, with the right index, the Server goes straight to the data the user wants. What is the right index? It is the column which tends to show up in the WHERE clause of many queries against the table. When you are designing a database for an application that frequently queries by certain columns, it is a good idea to create an index on that column, using the CREATE INDEX command.

For example, suppose you have an electronic employee directory which accesses information stored in an Oracle7 database. By typing in a fellow employee's last name or userid, users can find out other information about that person, such as the phone number and office location. You anticipate that most people will query by last name: underlying their queries is a statement similar to the following:

```
SQL> SELECT *
  2  FROM org
  3  WHERE last_name = 'Tallent';
```

To prepare for such queries, you create an index on the LAST_NAME column:

```
SQLDBA> CREATE INDEX org_lname_index
  ON org (last_name);
```

As a result, users querying by last name get information more quickly than users querying by an unindexed column, such as USERID.

One column that tends to show up in the WHERE clause is the primary key. Because of this tendency, the Server automatically creates an index on that column. This means that you don't have to create an index on the primary key. For example, since EMP_ID is the primary key for ORG, users querying by employee number will get a fast response because the Server has indexed the table on that column.

HASH CLUSTERS

While there are two types of clusters—indexed clusters and hash clusters—this section only discusses the latter because the use of hash clusters generally offers greater performance gains than the use of index clusters.

Clusters are sets of one or more tables in which related rows are physically stored near each other—in other words, related rows are either in one block or several contiguous blocks. For example, rows in a table that stores employees and their job titles might be grouped by job title, so that all employees of one job title will be stored together in one area, while employees of another job title will be stored together in another area. As with indexes, the idea is to enable quick access through the column in the WHERE clause.

How Hash Clusters Work

To see how hash clusters work, you need to understand some terms. A *cluster key* is the column by which you want to cluster. For example, suppose your table has a CODE column which frequently appears in the WHERE clause of exact match-queries (such as 'WHERE code = 537'). The CODE column is a good candidate for a cluster key.

In order to distribute all the cluster key values evenly, the Server applies a *hash function* to the cluster key values. Applying a hash function yields a *hash value* for each cluster key value. (Figure 9.4) For example, if you have 100 different codes, and you apply the hash function to each of them, you might get 25 different hash values.

When you create a hash cluster, you specify both the cluster key and the number of *hash keys*, or unique hash values. For example, the following command creates a cluster with 10 hash keys:

```
SQL> CREATE CLUSTER jobs_cluster (job_title CHAR(20))
  2   SIZE 24K
  3   HASHKEYS 10;
```

The SIZE parameter tells the Server how much space to allocate for storing all the rows in each hash key. We chose 24K in this case because we anticipate that each hash key will contain 12 rows of approximately 2K each.

After creating a cluster, you create a table and specify that it goes in the hash cluster. The following command, for example, creates the ORG table in the cluster we just created:

Cluster key values   **Hash key values**   **Hash keys**

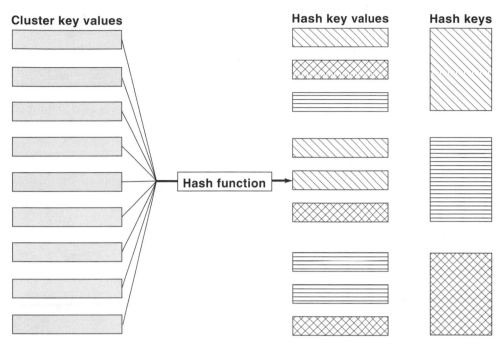

FIGURE 9.4 Applying a hash function to a cluster key value yields a hash value,
which corresponds to one of a prewset number of hash keys.

```
SQL> CREATE TABLE org
  2  (.
  3  .
  4  job_title    CHAR(20))
  5  CLUSTER jobs_cluster (job_title);
```

When a user inserts a row in the table, the Server applies the hash function to
the cluster key, determining which block should store the row.

Then, when another user queries by a cluster key value, the Server applies
the hash function to the cluster key value specified in the WHERE clause and
yields that row's hash key value, thus locating the block containing the row. For
example, consider a query from a user who wants to find the names of all the engineers in her company:

```
SQL> SELECT last_name, first_name
  2  FROM org
  3  WHERE job_title = 'ENGINEER';
```

To process this query, the Server applies its hash function to 'ENGINEER' to
determine which block or blocks store the rows with that cluster key value.

Knowing all this, you can see why storing data in a hash cluster results in
faster queries than using an index. With an index, the Server must read the index
in search of the indexed value and then read the appropriate block in the table.

With a hash cluster, the Server simply applies the hash function to the cluster key value and then reads the appropriate block. Thus, a query that uses a hash cluster requires only one I/O, as compared to the two or more required to use an index.

Choosing a Hash Function

If you want the Server to apply its own, internal hash function to your cluster key values, then use the CREATE CLUSTER syntax shown above. The Server will automatically use a hash function that distributes the cluster key values among the number of hash keys you specified, regardless of the datatype of the function.

But suppose you want each cluster key value to yield a unique hash value, so that applying the hash function will make the Server zero in on the exact row specified in the query's WHERE clause. If this is the case, then use the HASH IS clause when creating the cluster and specify a value for HASHKEYS that is at least as great as the number of different values in the cluster key.

For example, suppose you have a sequence that generates unique purchase order numbers for a table you want to create for a purchasing application. Since you expect users to search the database using the purchase order number, you create the following cluster:

```
SQL> CREATE CLUSTER po_cluster (po_number NUMBER(4))
  2    SIZE 2K
  3    HASH IS po_number
  4    HASHKEYS 10000;
```

Notice that the SIZE here is relatively small because each hash key will contain only a single row.

You can use the HASH IS option only if the values of the cluster key are non-negative integers. Furthermore, if you want to use the HASH IS option but specify a HASHKEYS value that is less than some of the cluster key values that will be in the cluster, then the cluster key values should be evenly spaced apart, ideally in a sequence. That way, the resulting hash values will be equally distributed among the hash keys.

Such even distribution is always important with hash clusters because the size of all hash keys is fixed (through the SIZE parameter). Uneven distribution of hash values means that some rows will not fit in the blocks set aside for a "popular" hash key, thus forcing these rows to be stored elsewhere. This phenomenon, of course, defeats the purpose of hash clusters because extra I/O will be required to scan those extra data blocks.

As with other topics discussed in this chapter, using hash clusters effectively is not a simple matter, and this discussion should serve only as a starting point for further reading and exploration.

SECURITY

CHAPTER OVERVIEW

An important part of a DBA's job is to control who has access to various databases. You do not want unauthorized users tampering with data in the database, and you want to control who sees what information. But database security goes beyond simply controlling read and write permissions. In this chapter, we discuss how you can use the Oracle Server to control exactly how different users can access the database.

IDENTIFICATION AND AUTHENTICATION

Central to security is the concept of identification. A user of a secure system—whether it be an operating system, an email account, or a database management system such as the Oracle Server—must have an identity that's maintained throughout the user's session. Like many other systems, the Oracle Server implements identification through usernames. Before a user can access an Oracle database, somebody (generally the DBA) must have created a username for that user.

Identification is important not only for access control decisions—such as whether a particular person can connect to an instance—but also for audit purposes. A username is like a unique footprint that a person leaves on the database's audit trail, making it possible for you to see who did what.

Clearly, identification is an important part of security. But a username alone, however, is not enough. A secure system must make sure that someone logging in under a particular username is, in fact, the person for whom the username was created. If a username were enough to connect to an instance, then anybody—including malicious outsiders—could connect. A method of authenticating users, therefore, is critical to security.

CREATING USERS

To create a user, you can issue the SQL command CREATE USER:

```
SQLDBA> CREATE USER wcather
              IDENTIFIED BY myantonia;
```

Alternatively, you can use a graphical database-administration utility. In SQL*DBA's screen mode, choosing Security > Create User brings up a dialog box in which you type all the attributes for the user.

When a user tries to connect to the Oracle Server, either the Server or the operating system can authenticate the user.

CHOOSING AN AUTHENTICATION METHOD

You specify whether authentication happens through the Oracle Server or through the operating system when you create a user. Therefore, it's possible for some users to be authenticated by the Server while others are authenticated by the operating system.

Server Authentication

If you choose Server authentication, then you must specify a password for the username. The database password can be the same as or different from the user's operating system password.

To use this authentication method, issue the CREATE USER command with the IDENTIFIED BY clause followed by the password, as in the example above.

OS Authentication

The alternative to Server authentication is OS authentication. As the DBA, you benefit from using OS authentication because it means that you do not have to do much to manage users: the operating system does it all. If you are both the DBA and the system administrator, then you only have to assign passwords once. The advantage to users is that they do not have to type in a password each time they connect to an instance.

Encrypted Passwords

Version 7.1 of the Oracle Server introduces extra security features, particularly for using the Server over a network.

When a user tries to connect to an instance on another machine, there's a risk that her password might be intercepted along the way. This is because even though passwords are stored in encrypted format, they are ordinarily sent across in clear-text format. To avoid this security hazard, DBAs using Version 7.1 can tell the Server to encrypt passwords before sending them over a network, using a different encryption algorithm from the one used to store passwords in the database. When the encrypted password reaches the remote machine, the Oracle Server authenticates it by comparing it to the password in the database.

Version 7.1 also lets DBAs securely administer remote databases through the use of a password file, which is also encrypted.

The disadvantage of using operating system authentication is that it eliminates one layer of protection. A malicious trespasser who succeeds in logging in to another user's operating system account can tap into the database as if he were the real user. If, however, Server authentication is used, the trespasser must crack the database password, as well.

To use this authentication method, issue the CREATE USER command with the IDENTIFIED EXTERNALLY clause:

```
SQLDBA> CREATE USER ops$dlodge
            IDENTIFIED EXTERNALLY;
```

Notice the OPS$ prefix before the operating system username DLODGE. Because Version 6 of the Oracle Server did not have the CREATE USER...IDENTIFIED EXTERNALLY syntax, the OPS$ prefix was required to specify operating-system authentication. For full backward compatibility with Version 6, Oracle7 gives users created with an OPS$ prefix all the rights of users created this way on Version 6 instances. For example, in Version 6, users with the OPS$ prefix could connect to a remote server by specifying a password. In the same way, OPS$ users created with Version 7 can connect to remote databases.

If maintaining Version 6 authentication behavior is not important to you, then you don't have to use the OPS$ prefix for operating system authentication. In fact, this prefix can be any string (even no string at all), but it must match the value of the initialization parameter OS_AUTHENT_PREFIX. For example, if you edited

your parameter file and gave OS_AUTHENT_PREFIX the value "x_", then the
CREATE USER statement should be the following:

```
SQLDBA> CREATE USER x_dlodge
              IDENTIFIED EXTERNALLY;
```

Regardless of whether you use operating-system authentication, the Server
takes over security management once the user has been allowed to connect to the
Server.

SETTING RESOURCE LIMITS THROUGH PROFILES

You can set resource limits on your users, controlling how many sessions they can
create, how many data blocks they can read per session, how long a session can
stay idle before disconnecting, and so on.

Creating a Profile

To group a set of resource limits, you must create a *profile*. For example, you
might decide to create three different profiles, one with low resource limits for all
parameters, one with high resource limits, and one with medium resource limits.
Or you might create profiles that are directly tied to various users' job functions.
For example, to create a profile to be used by students contending for scarce
resources in a database programming class, you might issue the following command:

```
SQL> CREATE PROFILE db_student LIMIT
   2   SESSIONS_PER_USER1
   3   CONNECT_TIME       50
   4   IDLE_TIME          10;
```

Assigning a Profile

Once you've created a profile, you can assign it to the appropriate users. If
you have not created the user, you can specify the profile as part of the CREATE
USER command:

```
SQLDBA> CREATE USER dlsayers
              IDENTIFIED BY gaudynight
              PROFILE db_student;
```

If you've already created the user, you can use the ALTER USER command
to specify the profile:

```
SQLDBA> ALTER USER wcather
              PROFILE db_student;
```

To make the Server enforce resource limits, you must set the value of the initialization parameter RESOURCE_LIMIT to TRUE.

Using the DEFAULT Profile

The example of the CREATE PROFILE command above does not specify values for all parameters. For example, it does not mention CPU_PER_SESSION or LOGICAL_READS_PER_SESSION, both of which are valid parameters. When you don't specify certain parameters, the Server uses values specified for those parameters in the database's default profile, called DEFAULT. If you have not altered this profile, then the value of each of its parameters is UNLIMITED. In other words, if you don't alter the DEFAULT profile, and you omit certain CREATE PROFILE parameters, you are implicitly telling the Oracle Server not to limit the use of those resources by the users having that profile.

The Server also uses the DEFAULT profile for users who were not explicitly assigned a profile.

DROPPING USERS

The opposite of creating users is dropping them. When you have created a user who should no longer have access to a particular database, you can drop that user by using either the SQL command DROP USER or a database administration utility:

```
SQLDBA> DROP USER wcather;
```

If WCATHER hasn't created any objects, her schema is empty and this command drops her as a user. If, however, she has objects in her schema, the only way to drop this user is to add the CASCADE clause:

```
SQLDBA> DROP USER wcather CASCADE;
```

Dropping a user this way means more than just cutting off that user's access to the database. Just as creating a user creates a schema for the user, so dropping a user with the CASCADE clause removes all objects in the user's schema. For example, if the user has created tables, then dropping the user drops all those tables.

You may not want this to happen. Jane Rand may go to work for a competitor, but that doesn't mean the work she's done at your company should necessarily be dropped. While you no longer want Jane to have access to the database, you want the objects she has created to remain. (Using DROP USER without the CASCADE clause will not work because the command only works if the schema is empty.) To keep the objects but remove her access, do not drop the user JRAND. Instead, revoke the CREATE SESSION privilege from JRAND:

```
SQLDBA> REVOKE CREATE SESSION
           FROM jrand;
```

Revoking the CREATE SESSION privilege prevents the user from connecting to the Oracle Server. Thus, even if the user owns objects in a particular database, revoking the CREATE SESSION command effectively prevents the user from accessing those objects.

GETTING INFORMATION ABOUT USERS

Information about users gets stored in the data dictionary and is available to DBAs through the DBA_USERS view. This view stores the usernames, encrypted passwords, and other information specified while creating or altering a user. If you just want to see all the users that were created for the database currently mounted, simply use the following command:

```
SQL> SELECT username
  2   FROM dba_users;
```

The following section explains more about granting and revoking privileges.

PRIVILEGES

Creating a user creates a schema for the user. By default, each user has access to objects in that user's schema. For example, user GEERTZ has access to the GEERTZ schema. But in order to have access to other objects, the user must have a privilege.

A *privilege* is a right to perform a certain operation. The Oracle Server has many different privileges to control everything from the creation of schema objects to the granting of privileges to other users.

The set of privileges that a user has, along with other settings specified when creating a user, is called the user's *security domain*. The security domain includes not only those privileges that have been explicitly granted to the user but also privileges the user has received through *roles*, which we will discuss later in this chapter.

TYPES OF PRIVILEGES

Oracle Server privileges are classified into two types: system privileges and object privileges. An *object privilege* is the right to perform an operation on a specific schema object. A *system privilege* is the right to perform an operation in general.

System Privileges

Here's a list of some system privileges:

❑ Create Any Cluster
❑ Create Database Link

❏ Alter Any Index

❏ Grant Any Privilege

❏ Drop Any Procedure

❏ Create Role

❏ Select Any Sequence

❏ Alter Session

❏ Drop Any Synonym

❏ Alter Any Table

❏ Select Any Table

❏ Drop Tablespace

❏ Create User

This list is only intended to give you a sense of the types of system privileges available. In reality, Oracle7 comes with more than 75 system privileges.

Object Privileges

Because of their nature, it's impossible to provide a complete list of object privileges: since each database consists of a unique set of schema objects, each database also has a unique set of object privileges.

A list of object privileges for the ORG table, for example, would include the privilege to create an index on ORG or to ALTER the table. It would also include the privileges to UPDATE the table, INSERT rows into the table, and DELETE rows from the table.

You do not have to have a system privilege to use an object privilege. For example, you don't need the INSERT ANY TABLE system privilege in order to insert rows into ORG. All you need is the INSERT privilege on the ORG table.

GRANTING PRIVILEGES

As you might guess, *granting* a privilege means giving a privilege to another user.

Granting Object Privileges

By default, you can only grant an object privilege to an object that you own. The exception to this rule is if you don't own the object but were given the GRANT OPTION on it.

For example, suppose LEONG owns the table LEONG_DATA. Leong wants Minsky to be the only other user who can view the table. Leong therefore issues the following statement:

```
SQL> GRANT SELECT
  2   ON leong_data
  3   TO minsky;
```

Once Leong has issued this command, Minsky can issue SELECTs on LEONG_DATA, but he cannot grant the same privilege to anyone else. (Leong, as the table owner, can of course grant the SELECT privilege to anybody else.)

But now suppose that Leong wants to give Minsky the right to not only see the data but also to grant others the same privilege. In this case, he issues the following command:

```
SQL> GRANT SELECT
  2  ON leong_data
  3  TO minsky
  4  WITH GRANT OPTION;
```

Instead of granting access to a whole table, like in the two examples above, you can grant an object privilege on specific columns in the table. For example, suppose Leong wants to give Minsky the right to update parts of LEONG_DATA, but not the whole table. To give Minsky the privilege to only update the WEIGHT and VOLUME columns (in addition to the privilege to view any part of the table), Leong issues the following statement:

```
SQL> GRANT SELECT,
  2  UPDATE (weight, volume)
  3  ON leong_data
  4  TO minsky;
```

The ability to issue this kind of statement allows you a finer granularity of security control over objects.

Granting System Privileges

To grant a system privilege, you must have either the GRANT ANY PRIVILEGE privilege or you must have the corresponding system privilege with the ADMIN OPTION. The ADMIN OPTION is to system privileges what the GRANT OPTION is to object privileges.

For example, suppose you have the ALTER SESSION privilege. You want to give it to another user, ARJUNA, with the option that Arjuna can give it to other users as well. To achieve this goal, you enter the following command:

```
SQLDBA> GRANT ALTER SESSION
              TO arjuna
              WITH ADMIN OPTION;
```

If you are using SQL*DBA in screen mode, you enable the ADMIN OPTION just by checking the box next to "Allow grantee to grant the privilege(s)/role(s) to others."

Using Views for Security

If you want to grant a user access to only part of a table, you can do it easily with a view. First, create a view consisting of the columns you want the user to be able to access. Then, grant the appropriate privileges to the view.

This method is more powerful and sometimes simpler than granting object privileges on specific columns of the base table. For example, if you want to give another user access to the same three columns for all SELECT, UPDATE, and INSERT operations, it makes sense to create a view on those three columns and then grant full SELECT, UPDATE, and INSERT privileges on the view. That way, you don't have to specify the same columns after each operation that you grant on the original table.

The reason views are often more powerful than object privileges is that they give you a finer level of control over which part of the object users can access. Because a view is defined by a query, you can create a view as any set of rows and columns. For example, if you want employees in the Engineering department to be able to select only data about employees in the same department, you could issue the following statement:

```
SQL> CREATE VIEW eng_view AS
  2  SELECT last_name, first_name, phone, dept
  3  FROM org
  4  WHERE dept = 'Engineering';
```

Then, you could give all the users in Engineering the SELECT object privilege on all of ENG_VIEW.

Now suppose that instead of SELECT, you also want to grant users the right to UPDATE and INSERT rows. If you simply grant the appropriate object privileges on the view you've defined, however, users would be able to insert rows into the base table via that view, even if the new rows do not have "Engineering" in the DEPT column. To prevent this "back-door" way of inserting data, you can create the same view with the CHECK OPTION:

```
SQL> CREATE VIEW eng_view2 AS
  2  SELECT last_name, first_name, phone, dept
  3  FROM org
  4  WHERE dept = 'Engineering'
  5  WITH CHECK OPTION;
```

(Continued on next page)

Using Views for Security (Continued)

As a result of the constraint in line 5, users granted INSERT or UPDATE privileges on ENG_VIEW2 can only make changes that result in rows that the view can select. For example, users could not insert a row in which the value of DEPT is "Marketing," because the subquery for ENG_VIEW2 only selects rows where the value of DEPT is "Engineering."

Because views are based on subqueries, they enable you to use SQL's special functions. For example, if you want to create a generic version of ENG_VIEW (such that an employee in any department could only see data for his or her own department) you could use the USER function, which returns the username of the user who is logged in:

```
SQL> CREATE VIEW emp_view_generic AS
  2    SELECT last_name, first_name, phone, dept
  3    FROM org
  4    WHERE dept = (SELECT dept FROM org
  5            WHERE user_id = USER);
```

Using the SYSDATE function in the definition of a view, you can specify when users can access the data in the view. Consider the following view:

```
SQL> CREATE VIEW wage_view_weekdays AS
  2    SELECT emp_id, salary
  3    FROM wages
  4    WHERE TO_CHAR(SYSDATE,'D') BETWEEN 2 AND 6;
```

Queries of this view can only occur between Monday and Friday. Don't be concerned with the syntax of these queries; just keep in mind the possibilities that views offer.

REVOKING PRIVILEGES

To revoke, or take away, privileges from other users, you must have at least the same privileges as those you'd need to grant privileges.

Revoking Object Privileges

To revoke object privileges, you must actually have granted the privilege you are revoking. For example, hundreds of users may have the SELECT privilege on ORG; six of these users may have this privilege with the GRANT OPTION. But only one user can revoke this privilege from any given user. So if

WCATHER granted the privilege to MTWAIN, only WCATHER can revoke the privilege from MTWAIN, even though there are five other users who could grant the same privilege.

Furthermore, revoking an object privilege from a user who had the GRANT OPTION has a cascading effect: users who had been granted the object privilege by the user from whom you revoke the privilege automatically get their privileges revoked as well.

Revoking System Privileges

These rules do not hold true for system privileges. To revoke a system privilege from another user, you only need to have that privilege with the ADMIN OPTION—you don't have to have granted the system privilege. Revoking a system privilege does *not* have a cascading effect: users who had been granted a system privilege by a user with the ADMIN OPTION maintain their privileges after that user's system privilege is revoked.

How to Revoke Privileges

You can revoke privileges with the REVOKE command. For example, to revoke the ALTER SESSION privilege from ARJUNA, enter the following command:

```
SQLDBA> REVOKE ALTER SESSION
            FROM arjuna;
```

Revoking a privilege takes effect the next time the user needs the privilege. For example, if a user is logged in and you revoke the CREATE SESSION privilege, the user will remain logged in because once the session has been created, the Server does not require the CREATE SESSION privilege. When the user logs out and tries to connect again, though, the Server will check privileges and the user will not be able to connect.

Notice that you do not have to specify that you are revoking the ADMIN OPTION that this privilege had attached to it. Revoking a privilege takes it away completely, including of course the option associated with it.

GRANTING PRIVILEGES ON PROGRAM UNITS

An effective way to reduce the number of privileges explicitly granted to users is to grant users the EXECUTE privilege on whatever stored procedures, functions, or packages they need to call. A user with the EXECUTE privilege on a stored procedure that creates a new student record, for example, does not need privileges on the STUDENTS table. The procedure works because it runs with the privileges of the user who created it, not of the user who calls it.

Granting the EXECUTE privilege on a program unit is similar to granting any other object privilege:

```
SQLDBA> GRANT EXECUTE
            ON create_student
            TO arjuna;
```

Another benefit of granting EXECUTE on program units rather than on specific objects is that you can precisely limit what the user will be able to do. The user will only be able to access objects through the program unit—not through ad hoc SQL statements—and thus will be less likely to do something not intended by the programmer or the DBA.

GETTING INFORMATION ABOUT PRIVILEGES

Two data dictionary views are useful for getting information about privileges granted to users and roles: DBA_SYS_PRIVS and DBA_COL_PRIVS.

For each user or role (defined in a later section) that has been granted a system privilege, DBA_SYS_PRIVS stores the grantee, the name of the privilege, and whether the privilege was granted with the ADMIN OPTION. To see all of this information for your database, use the following query:

```
SQL> SELECT *
  2   FROM dba_sys_privs;
```

Similarly, for each user who has been granted an object privilege, DBA_COL_PRIVS stores information about the privilege—including the name of the table, the name of the column, the type of privilege, and so on. To see all the object privileges granted to WCATHER, for example, use the following query:

```
SQL> SELECT table_name, column_name, privilege, grantable
  2   FROM dba_col_privs
  3   WHERE grantee = 'wcather';
```

ROLES

A new feature of Oracle7 is role-based security. A *role* is a set of privileges that has a name and can be assigned to either users or to other roles.

HOW DO ROLES WORK?

A DBA—or any user with the CREATE ROLE privilege—can create any role, for example: CLERK, MANAGER, BUYER, REPORTER, and so on, and associate various privileges with those roles. Once those roles are defined, you can grant any number of roles to a user, thus granting that user all the privileges associated with those roles.

Creating a Role

You create a role in the same way as you create a user, by giving the role a name and a password:

```
SQLDBA> CREATE ROLE accountant
           IDENTIFIED BY ilikenumbers;
```

If you create a role with a password and don't assign that role as the default role for the user, then the user will have to specify the password when he enables the role. If you don't want this extra password-checking, you can create a role without a password:

```
SQLDBA> CREATE ROLE accountant
           NOT IDENTIFIED;
```

Defining the Role

After creating the role, assign privileges to the role by using the GRANT command (or its SQL*DBA equivalent):

```
SQLDBA> GRANT SELECT, INSERT, UPDATE
           ON finance
           TO accountant;
```

As you can see, the syntax for giving privileges to a role is the same as for granting privileges to a user.

In a separate command, you can assign some system privileges to the role. For example, all users who will have the role will need the CREATE SESSION privilege:

```
SQLDBA> GRANT CREATE SESSION
           TO accountant;
```

This separate statement is necessary because you cannot grant system and object privileges in the same command.

Granting the Role

Now that the role has been created and defined in terms of its privileges, you can grant it to users or other roles.

For example, to grant the ACCOUNTANT role to DLODGE, WCATHER, and MTWAIN, use the following command:

```
SQLDBA> GRANT accountant
           TO dlodge, wcather, mtwain;
```

This command is the equivalent of granting each of those users all the system and object privileges associated with the ACCOUNTANT role.

You can also grant a role to another role, just like you can grant a role to a user. For example, suppose that in addition to the ACCOUNTANT privileges, you want users who are accountants to have all the privileges that bookkeepers have. If you have defined the role BOOKKEEPER, you simply grant that role to the ACCOUNTANT role:

```
SQLDBA> GRANT bookkeeper
           TO accountant;
```

In addition, you can assign several roles to one user and can add privileges on top of the roles. Thus, any user's security domain might consist of multiple roles and any privileges directly granted to the user.

Enabling the Role

After you have granted a role to a user, the user does not immediately get all the privileges of that role. To enable a role for himself or herself, the user must issue the SET ROLE command, specifying which role to enable. For example, to enable ACCOUNTANT, DLODGE can issue the following statement:

```
SQL> SET ROLE accountant
  2   IDENTIFIED BY ilikenumbers;
```

The exception to this requirement that a user must explicitly enable a role is the user's default role or roles. In other words, even if a default role is password-protected, a user does not have to give a password to receive the role: the user receives it automatically when creating a session.

To enable all one's roles, a user can issue the following command:

```
SQL> SET ROLE ALL;
```

In both cases, the SET ROLE command only enables the roles for the current session. If the user disconnects from the Server and reconnects again, the roles will again be disabled. To enable a set of roles for a user each time the user connects, the DBA or application developer can either create default roles for a user or enable the roles through an application that accesses the Server.

If you use the second approach, the application issues a SET ROLE statement on startup. Thus, any user that can start the application automatically gets all the privileges needed to run the application, but loses other privileges that user may have had enabled.

The other way to have a set of roles automatically enabled each time a user logs in is to define default roles for the user. If you create the roles after creating the users, you must use the ALTER USER statement to give the user a set of default roles:

```
SQLDBA> ALTER USER wcather
              DEFAULT ROLE accountant;
```

As a result of this command, each time WCATHER connects to the Server she will have all the privileges of the ACCOUNTANT role.

Revoking Privileges from a Role

You have already learned that you can revoke a privilege from a user if you granted the privilege directly, not through a role. You can only revoke directly granted privileges from a user. So how do you revoke a privilege that a user only has as part of a role?

One way is to revoke the role, but doing so of course revokes all the other privileges that are part of that role. Another way is to revoke the undesired privilege from the role, but doing that affects all other users who have that privilege. Therefore, if you want to reduce a user's security domain, the best solution is to revoke the old role, create a new (less privileged) role, and assign the new role to the user.

WHY USE ROLES WHEN YOU CAN USE PRIVILEGES?

Using roles makes security management easier and faster than assigning individual privileges to users. Roles especially make sense when groups of users need the same privileges. For example, if all purchasing agents need the same privileges, it makes sense to create a role—say, BUYER—and grant the necessary privileges to that role. Then you can grant the role to all the employees in the purchasing department. This takes fewer commands than assigning all the necessary privileges to buyer A, then buyer B, then to buyer C, and so on. (Figure 10.1)

Roles are also easier to maintain than privileges. If the responsibilities of an entire department change, you only have to change the definition of the role, instead of having to grant or revoke privileges for every user in the department. Similarly, if a user transfers from one department to another, you only have to revoke the old role and grant the new one; without roles, you would have to revoke a whole set of privileges one by one, and assign a new set one by one.

PREDEFINED ROLES

You can create any role you want and assign it any name that has not been taken up by another role or user. The number of different roles is limited only by the number of possible combinations of object privileges and system privileges for a particular database.

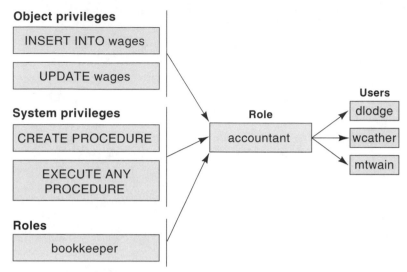

FIGURE 10.1 A single role consolidates multiple privileges, making it easier to grant privileges to users.

In addition, for compatibility between Version 6 and Version 7, the Oracle7 Server comes with three predefined roles: CONNECT, RESOURCE, and DBA. The DBA role consists of all system privileges with the ADMIN OPTION, so that a user who has been granted the DBA role can grant any system privileges to other users or roles.

In general, though, it is better to create your own roles instead of using predefined ones. For example, the team of DBAs working in your corporation do not all need the full set of DBA privileges. Therefore, the main DBA can create roles for different DBA functions: one role might have all privileges required to create new users; another role could have all the privileges necessary to back up a database; a third role might have the privileges for creating databases, and so on. Instead of giving each DBA the DBA role, the main DBA can grant each DBA the role necessary to perform that employee's job functions.

Granting predefined roles, in contrast, gives users more privileges than they might need and can jeopardize the security of your database.

GETTING INFORMATION ABOUT ROLES

Two data dictionary views are useful for getting information about roles: DBA_ROLES and DBA_ROLE_PRIVS.

DBA_ROLES simply stores the names of all the roles in the database, along with whether a password is required to enable the role. To see all the roles in the database, use the following query:

```
SQL> SELECT role
  2  FROM dba_roles;
```

A related view, DBA_ROLE_PRIVS, stores which roles have been granted to various users and to other roles. To see a list of users (and roles) that have been granted roles, along with the names of the roles granted, use the following query:

```
SQL> SELECT grantee, granted_role
  2  FROM dba_role_privs;
```

FILE PERMISSIONS

Even though object and system privileges control what database operations various users can perform, it is also important to set the file permissions correctly on the operating system files that users will be accessing.

In a relational database system, users access data through an intermediary, such as the Oracle Server, instead of reading files directly. Therefore, you must ensure that file permissions are set in such a way as to prevent users from reading or writing to a database file directly.

All database files, therefore, should be set so that only the file owner (that is, the DBA) has read and write permission. Optionally, you can also grant read permission to other DBAs in your group. But other users should have no read or write permission. Oracle processes, by virtue of being started by the same user who has read and write permission to the data, log, and control files (that is, the DBA), will be able to read from and write to the database files on behalf of users and applications. For example, on UNIX systems, the database server process runs with setuid to **oracle**, oracle being the only operating system account that needs access to the physical database files. In this way, you allow users to access the database files only through the Oracle Server.

AUDITING DATABASE ACTIVITY

Even if you have taken proper measures to secure your database, security problems might occur. To become quickly aware of these problems and to find their cause, you need to audit database activity.

The Oracle Server gives you a wide range of options over what activity to audit. After all, an audit trail can easily become too long and cluttered to be of much use. Basically, you can choose to audit particular SQL statements, such as all DELETE statements or all UPDATE statements; you can choose to audit all statements requiring a particular system privilege, such as the DROP ANY

Storing Classified Information with Trusted Oracle7

For extra security, such as required by some government agencies, Oracle Corporation offers a special version of the Oracle Server called Trusted Oracle. In addition to all the features of the regular Oracle Server, Trusted Oracle provides multilevel security, helping to manage data of different sensitivities.

To determine who sees various pieces of data, Trusted Oracle uses mandatory access control. With mandatory access control, database objects have labels indicating their sensitivity or classification. Each user also has a label that mandates to what sensitivity of information the user has read or write access. To access a particular object, a user of a Trusted Oracle database must have both the appropriate object privileges and the label corresponding to the sensitivity of the object.

Thus, you can think of Trusted Oracle as an extra layer of security, because it uses all the regular security features of the Oracle Server and tightened measures as well. Trusted Oracle7 provides a level of security that corresponds to Level B1 of the Trusted Computer Systems Evaluation Criteria (TCSEC), while standard Oracle7 corresponds to TCSEC Level C2.

PROCEDURE privilege. You can choose to audit only unsuccessful attempts to perform certain actions. Optionally, you can further narrow down your audit to a specific user or users.

For example, suppose after you analyze a broad audit trail, you suspect that BARNOLD or AAMES might be changing data in tables that users are not authorized to access. You can start a new audit trail using the following command:

```
SQLDBA> AUDIT UPDATE TABLE, DELETE TABLE, INSERT TABLE
          BY aames, barnold;
```

The audit trail that results from this statement will indicate which tables BARNOLD and AAMES are accessing.

Instead of auditing by a particular type of SQL statement, you can audit a specific schema object. For example, if you want to keep a record of all SELECT activity on the COURSES table in the schema PROF, you can use the following AUDIT command:

```
SQLDBA> AUDIT SELECT
          ON prof.courses;
```

One interesting auditing option is to track unsuccessful activity, because such activity might indicate that a user is trying to do something for which he is unauthorized. For example, to create an audit trail of unsuccessful attempts to UPDATE courses, issue the following command:

```
SQLDBA> AUDIT UPDATE
            ON prof.courses
            WHENEVER UNSUCCESSFUL;
```

To enable auditing during a particular instance, you must set the initialization parameter AUDIT_TRAIL to TRUE.

These examples show only some of the auditing options available through the Oracle Server. No matter which option you choose, the audit trail keeps a record of the following information for every statement audited:

❑ the username of the user who executed the statement

❑ the code indicating what type of statement it was

❑ the object referenced in the statement

❑ the time the statement was executed

Of course, creating good audit trails is only half the battle of spotting and rooting out unauthorized activity. You must also examine and analyze the audit trail.

To examine the audit trail, you can use one of several data dictionary views. For example, DBA_AUDIT_OBJECT stores trail records for all objects in the database.

BACKUP, FAILURE, AND RECOVERY

CHAPTER OVERVIEW

A database can be subject to many kinds of errors and failures in the course of day-to-day operations of the Server. Probably the most common type of failure that could jeopardize data integrity and consistency is instance failure, which might occur during a power outage or operating-system failure. Another common failure is media failure, whereby some piece of physical storage becomes unreadable or unwritable.

This chapter focuses on these two types of failure, describes ways that the Oracle Server safeguards data in such events, and examines what the DBA can do to facilitate fast and accurate recovery.

TYPES OF FAILURE

All the problems that can occur in a database that jeopardize the consistency and accuracy of data can be categorized into three areas. It's important to understand the three types of failures, because the type of failure determines what the DBA and the Server must do to recover the database from the failure.

USER PROCESS FAILURE

User process failure occurs when a user process, such as an application used to update an Oracle database, dies. This sort of failure can occur for many reasons. For example, the user might quit out of the application suddenly, without explicitly committing or rolling back changes. A network connection might break, halting the flow of data between the user and the Server, or a power failure affecting only the client could abort the user process. Whatever the cause, all such failures have one element in common: they affect only a single user process, leaving the Server intact.

Such a failure does jeopardize the consistency of the database, because the data buffers might contain modified data that the user has not committed. But because only one user process has died, only one incomplete transaction needs to be resolved. A single background process, PMON, can take care of this problem. At regular intervals, PMON checks for dead user processes. When it finds one, it rolls back that process's incomplete transaction using data in the rollback segment, thus bringing the database back to a consistent state. It also releases any locks held by the user process. All of this cleanup happens automatically, with no intervention by the DBA.

INSTANCE FAILURE

A more serious type of failure—because it affects more users and transactions—is instance failure. Instance failure occurs when the instance suddenly dies. It occurs when a DBA shuts down the instance with the Abort option, when someone kills a background process, or when the underlying operating system crashes. Clearly, a power outage that shuts down the machine on which the Server runs also causes an instance failure.

Because many user processes generally access a single instance, instance failure often results in many unresolved transactions. Recall that when a user issues a COMMIT, the transaction does not instantly get written to the data files. Instead, the redo information gets written to the online redo log file, while the transaction data itself remains in the database buffer cache until it is efficient for DBWR to write it to a data file. Under normal conditions, this deferred write does not create a consistency problem because—as noted in Chapter 6—the Server guarantees that users always retrieve consistent data, whether it be from the data files or the SGA. But when an instance fails, the SGA— including the database buffer cache—disappears. And since the SGA is gone, DBWR cannot write modified data buffers, for either committed or uncommitted transactions, to the data files.

The only way to recover that lost data is to get it from the redo log files. This is something the Server does as part of instance recovery, a process which, like process recovery, requires no work on the part of the DBA. We will discuss how the Server performs recovery after an instance failure later in this chapter.

MEDIA FAILURE

Media failure occurs when a storage medium such as a disk crashes or becomes corrupted, causing the loss of data on the medium. Depending on which disk crashes, media failure destroys either a data file, a redo log file, or a control file. Unwittingly deleting a file also constitutes a media failure.

Media failure causes a loss of data that is more difficult to recreate because physical files, rather than temporary processes and memory buffers, disappear. Because physical files disappear, media failure causes a loss of data that is more difficult to recover than data lost due to instance failure. Recovering from media failure, therefore, requires intervention on the part of the DBA.

BACKUP

Regularly backing up your database is the only way to restore the database after a media failure.

HOW BACKUP MAKES FULL RECOVERY POSSIBLE

If you've worked with a word processor and backed up your document to a floppy disk, you're halfway to understanding how the Oracle Server recovers data. In the case of your word processor, if the hard disk you were working on crashed, you would need to restore your document using the copy on the floppy disk. Having used the floppy disk was a good idea because now you could get much of your work back. You can't get all of your work back because chances are you did some work after you made the backup.

In the case of the Oracle Server, you *can* get all of your work back. Getting back the first part of your work is called *restoring* it from backup. Getting back the second part—the part done after the last backup—is called *recovery*. While all this is fairly simple, it gets confusing because no separate term exists for the whole process, so people talk about recovery when they mean the combination of restoring and recovering. To avoid this confusion, this chapter uses the term *full recovery* when referring to the combined process. (Figure 11.1)

TYPES OF BACKUP

Databases that are not used around the clock can be backed up using an *offline* backup, sometimes called a *cold backup*. Some databases must always be available, so backing them up requires an *online* backup, sometimes called a *hot backup*.

PERFORMING OFFLINE BACKUPS

Oracle DBAs should perform regular backups of the database.

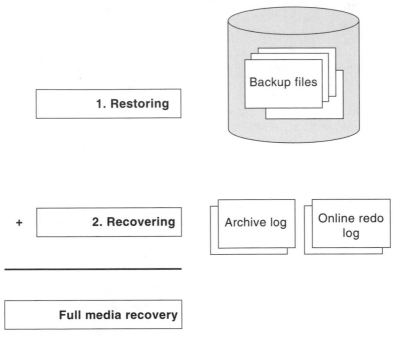

FIGURE 11.1 Full recovery involves restoring from backup and recovering from log files.

To perform an offline backup, you first shut down all instances accessing the database and close the database. Then, you use an operating-system utility to back up the data files and the initialization file. For example, if the files are on a UNIX system, you might use the **cpio** utility to copy the files.

Getting the Filenames

Before you begin backing up, you need to know the names of all the files. To find out the names of all the data files, query the appropriate data dictionary view. For example, to find the names of the data files, issue the following command:

```
SQLDBA> SELECT file_name
            FROM sys.dba_data_files;
```

To find the names of the log files, use the following command:

```
SQLDBA> SELECT member
            FROM sys.v$logfile;
```

To find the name of the control file, you can simply see the value of the initialization parameter CONTROL_FILES:

```
SQLDBA> SHOW PARAMETER control_files;
```

Using an Operating System Utility or Parallel Backup/Restore

On many operating systems, Oracle Corporation provides a product called Parallel Backup/Restore which can help you perform much faster backups (and restores) than operating-system utilities can.

Performing an offline backup allows you to create a full, consistent backup. All backed up files are consistent with respect to a single point in time, because no data is changing while any file is being backed up.

PERFORMING ONLINE BACKUPS

If you are making an online backup, you cannot back up all your files simultaneously but must back them up tablespace by tablespace.

Backing Up the Data Files

Before you begin your online backup of a particular tablespace, tell the Server when the backup is about to begin:

```
SQLDBA> ALTER TABLESPACE users
            BEGIN BACKUP;
```

This information tells the Server to mark this moment as the last consistent state. As a result of this command, the Server will know that in the case of a failure, it will have to apply redo information for any transactions that occur after this moment.

Having marked the start of the backup, you can begin copying the data files in that tablespace using an operating-system utility. (Recall from Chapter 8 that you can find out which data files a tablespace contains by querying the data dictionary view DBA_DATA_FILES with the tablespace name in the WHERE clause.)

Finish backing up the tablespace by telling the Server that you're done:

```
SQLDBA> ALTER TABLESPACE users
            END BACKUP;
```

Repeat this entire procedure for each tablespace that you want to back up.

Backing Up the Control File

After you have backed up all your data files, back up the control file using the ALTER DATABASE COMMAND. For example, to copy the control file for the currently open database to the /disk5/backup directory, enter the following command:

```
SQLDBA> ALTER DATABASE
               BACKUP CONTROLFILE TO '/disk5/backup/finance_b.ctl';
```

Backing Up the Initialization Parameter File

Finally, back up the initialization parameter file. Since this file does not get read or modified while an instance is running, you don't have to warn the Server that you will be backing it up. Simply copy it using the appropriate operating system utility.

Using a Script

As you can see, the procedure for making an online backup is more complicated than the one for an offline backup. Skipping any steps could produce an ineffective, perhaps useless, backup. Therefore, if you plan to make frequent online backups, consider writing a SQL script that automates the process.

Executing Operating System Commands from a SQL Script

If you want to perform a backup using a SQL script, you will need to issue some operating system commands from within the script. Since operating system commands are not part of SQL, however, you need to get the operating system to process them.

To get SQL*DBA or SQL*Plus to transfer control temporarily back to the operating system, precede your operating system command with the keyword "HOST." This SQL keyword tells the SQL interpreter that the command that follows is an operating system command.

Making Sure Consistency Is Not a Problem

You have learned that a complete offline backup generates a backup that is consistent with respect to a single point in time. But what about online backups? Since users are continuing to update files as you are copying them, the data on the backed up files is not consistent: part of a backup file might contain old data (that has been modified after the backup began) while another part might contain newer data (that reflects changes made after the backup began). This scenario is a variation of the problem of inconsistent reads discussed in Chapter 6.

As it turns out, this inconsistency is not a problem when it comes time to restore the database. True, the files initially restored are inconsistent. But when you perform the second step of full recovery—having the Server recover from log files—the data becomes consistent because the log files have a record of all the changes made during the course of backup.

Before the Server can apply all the redo entries for this period, though, it needs a redo log that goes back to that period. Therefore, you need to have been archiving your online redo log files, by running the instance in ARCHIVELOG mode (which we will discuss later in the chapter).

You can see now why the procedure for an online backup did not include a step for backing up redo log files: all online backups require the instance to be running with archiving enabled, thus creating a copy of the online redo log files.

FREQUENCY OF BACKUPS

The more frequently you make backups, the faster will be your recovery after media failure. Suppose you make backups once a week, on Sunday afternoon. If the disk containing your data files crashes on Friday afternoon, you will be able to *restore* the database to the state it was in on Sunday, just before you performed your last backup. Then, you will have to *recover* transactions made between Sunday and Friday by applying those changes from the archived redo log and the current redo log.

But if you make backups every evening, recovery is very fast because you can restore the database to its Thursday evening state. Then, you only have to apply the transactions made from Thursday evening until Friday's crash.

All this is not meant to suggest that daily backups are better than weekly or even monthly ones. Rather, the point is that recovery is faster with more frequent backups. (Figure 11.2) Furthermore, there's a trade-off between spending time making frequent backups and spending time recovering a database that has not been recently backed up. For example, making daily backups may not be worth the time if your database doesn't change frequently. How frequently you back up your database will depend largely on how frequently the data changes.

ANOTHER REASON TO CREATE A BACKUP

In general, a backup is only necessary for media failure—not instance or user process failure. In addition, though, it's a good practice to create a backup each time you make a change to the database's physical structure, just before making the change.

For example, if you are planning to rename a data file, you should back up the control file (which includes the old data file's specification) just before renaming the data file.

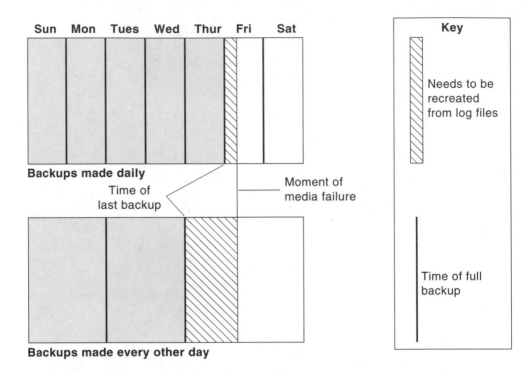

FIGURE 11.2 Making daily backups yields to quicker media recovery than making backups less frequently, like every other day.

RECOVERY

Whether you are recreating data after an instance failure or a media failure, part of the process involves recovery using the redo log files. If you experienced a media failure and have restored files from backup, you will want to recover transactions made after the backup. If you experienced an instance failure, you don't need to restore files and can begin recovery immediately.

The Oracle Server performs recovery automatically when you restart the instance. However, to prepare the Server for recovery, you need to create and properly place several recovery structures, namely the redo log files.

REDO LOG BUFFERS AND REDO LOG FILES

When a user makes a change, information about the change is stored in a redo log buffer in the SGA. When the user commits the change, information from the redo log buffer gets written to a redo log file. This way, if an instance failure occurs after the data is on disk, that data can be recovered because the Server can apply the redo information from the redo log files to the data files.

HOW MULTIPLE LOG FILES WORK TOGETHER

When you create a database, you specify two or more redo log files. The idea behind having multiple redo log files is that when one fills up, the Server can immediately begin writing to the second one.

To understand the need for multiple redo log files, imagine the problems of having just one redo log file. The LGWR would overwrite redo log entries at the beginning of the log file in order to store newer redo log entries, even if the older entries still contained data that is not yet on data files and therefore is critical to recovery. Or, to avoid this danger, the LGWR might wait until the data corresponding to the older redo log entries is safely on the data files, holding up transactions from being committed. (This is the approach used by other database servers: the servers made by Informix and Sybase only use one physical log file.) Either way, there's a problem: you need at least two redo log files.

So how do multiple log files work? Suppose you have two redo log files, A and B. (Figure 11.3) As users commit transactions, the LGWR moves redo entries from the SGA to A, to which it assigns a *log sequence number,* say 27. Once A fills up, LGWR begins writing to B, to which it assigns the next log sequence number, 28. This moment at which LGWR stops writing to one file and starts writing to another is called a *log switch.* Should a failure occur, and you restart the instance, the Server uses the first log, as indicated by the sequence number, and starts applying its redo entries in order of their system change number; it then proceeds to the second log, and so on.

If archiving is enabled, then a log switch also activates the ARCH background process: as soon as an online redo log file fills up, ARCH copies it to an archive redo log file.

Keep in mind that a log sequence number corresponds to a set of redo entries, not to a particular file. For example, once log B fills up, LGWR begins writing to log A, to which it now assigns log sequence number 29. So the same file that had entries belonging to log 27 now has entries belonging to set 29; therefore, the first file to which LGWR wrote may not be the first one from which the Server begins applying redo entries during recovery.

HOW THE SERVER PERFORMS RECOVERY

When you restart the failed instance, the Server uses the SMON background process to recover any transactions that the data files don't contain.

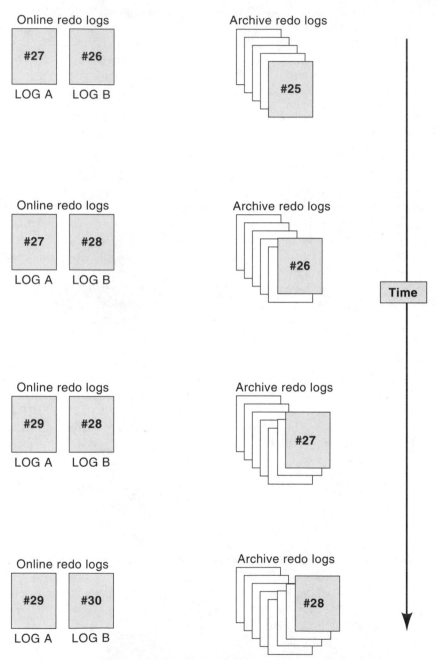

FIGURE 11.3 The log sequence number corresponds to the set of redo entries of a single redo log. After an online redo log fills up, ARCH copies it to an archive redo log if archiving is enabled.

Parallel Recovery

Another new feature of Version 7.1 is Parallel Recovery. This feature speeds up recovery by splitting up the work of applying changes from redo log files among several processes. To make maximum use of parallel recovery, your data needs to be spread among multiple data files on different disks.

To enable parallel recovery, you must set the number of parallel processes to be used for recovery in the RECOVERY_PARALLELISM initialization parameter.

Rolling Forward

The first thing SMON does is to *roll forward*, which means to apply to the data files all changes recorded in the redo log files.

Rolling Back

Though *rolling back* may sound like undoing all the work done by rolling forward, it actually means only undoing incomplete transactions.

The problem with merely stopping after rolling forward is that, as noted earlier, data files usually contain data that has not been committed. The purpose of rolling back, then, is to undo this uncommitted data from the data files, bringing the database to a consistent state.

Also, rolling back is necessary to undo any uncommitted transactions that got written to data files as a result of rolling forward. In general, the redo log contains completed transactions, but it sometimes has entries for changes that did not get committed when the failure occurred. (While LGWR ordinarily copies data to the log files only after a user has entered a COMMIT, it must occasionally write uncommitted data to make room in the log buffer.) These uncommitted transactions get applied to the data files during the roll forward phase of recovery, and must therefore be rolled back to maintain consistency.

Where does SMON get the rollback data? Some of this data, which gets stored in rollback segments on the data files, presumably got lost as a result of the failure. But remember that the redo log keeps information about *all* changes to the database, including changes to the rollback segments. Thus, the process of rolling forward also recovers the rollback segments. As a result, by the time SMON begins rolling back, the rollback segments have all the information necessary to roll back uncommitted transactions.

CHECKPOINTS

A database checkpoint is the moment the DBWR writes data from the SGA to the data files. This moment is significant for recovery because once data is on a data file, it does not need to be recovered from the redo log. Therefore, only changes made after the last checkpoint are applied during recovery.

When Do Checkpoints Occur?

By default, a checkpoint occurs during every log switch. That is, when a log file fills up, the DBWR also writes modified data to data files.

Remember, though, that in the case of instance failure, all data since the last checkpoint has to be recovered. Therefore, if you want recovery to occur as quickly as possible, you might want checkpoints to occur more frequently. You can force a checkpoint to occur after any number of seconds by setting the initialization parameter LOG_CHECKPOINT_TIMEOUT. Or, you can set the checkpoint interval in terms of the number of redo log blocks that have been filled since the last checkpoint by setting another initialization parameter, LOG_CHECKPOINT_INTERVAL. This parameter can be useful if your log files are large, which means that the time between log switches is too long.

ADDITIONAL STRUCTURES FOR FULL RECOVERY FROM MEDIA FAILURE

To protect against failure of media containing data files and failure of media containing log files, you need to enable both archiving and mirrored redo log files. Archived redo log files enable you to recover from a crash to the disk containing data files, while mirrored redo log files allow you to recover from a crash to the disk containing redo log files.

Some operating systems have their own mirroring mechanisms. The Oracle Server does not depend on these mechanisms. As long as you have enough disks, you can have the Oracle Server mirror your control file and redo log files—no matter what platform you are using to run the Server.

MIRRORED REDO LOG FILES

To protect against some types of media failure, you can choose to use *mirrored* redo log files. Mirrored redo log files are identical copies of redo log files kept on different disks. The two (or more) identical copies make up a *log group*, and each file in the group is called a *member*. (Figure 11.4) If one disk crashes, destroying one set of redo log files, the other disk will contain an identical set.

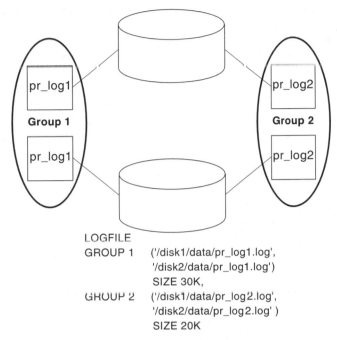

LOGFILE
GROUP 1   ('/disk1/data/pr_log1.log',
                  '/disk2/data/pr_log1.log')
                  SIZE 30K,
GROUP 2   ('/disk1/data/pr_log2.log',
                  '/disk2/data/pr_log2.log')
                  SIZE 20K

FIGURE 11.4 Mirrored files are identical copies of a file stored on different disks, to prepare for media failure.

When you create mirrored redo log files, you must make them the same size. That way, when a log switch occurs from one, it also occurs from the other, and the files will be exact duplicates of one another. This is so important that the syntax of the LOGFILE clause of the CREATE DATABASE command makes it impossible to create mirrored log files of different sizes:

```
SQLDBA> CREATE DATABASE pubrel
            LOGFILE GROUP 1 ('/disk1/data/pr_log1.log',
                    '/disk2/data/pr_log1.log') SIZE 30K,
                GROUP 2 ('/disk1/data/pr_log2.log',
                    '/disk2/data/pr_log2.log') SIZE 20K,
           .
           ;
```

Notice that the SIZE parameter applies to the whole group, so that both members of group 1 are 30K and both members of group 2 are 20K.

Mirrored redo log files are sometimes called *duplexed* or *multiplexed* redo logs.

MIRRORED CONTROL FILE

The control file is critical to any kind of recovery because it stores, among other information, the current log sequence number and the latest checkpoint. During recovery, the Server reads the control file to find out from which log it should start recovering and which redo entries on that log occurred after the last checkpoint. Without this information, accurate recovery is impossible. Therefore, the loss of this one small file is as detrimental as the loss of the entire database.

You will be backing up the control file during your regular backups. In addition, though, it is wise to keep a mirrored copy of the control file on another disk. This way, changes to the control file are instantly stored in two places, just as with mirrored redo log files.

ARCHIVED REDO LOG FILES

You can choose for all filled redo log files to be archived, or permanently copied, to another set of files so that when LGWR overwrites a redo log file, the information does not get lost. Each of the archive log files represents one online redo log file. After every log switch, ARCH creates an additional archive log file to store data from the filled redo log.

The Need for Archived Redo Log Files

Knowing that LGWR does not begin overwriting a redo log file until its transactions are on the data file, you might wonder why you'd ever want to choose archiving. But consider what happens if the disk containing the data files crashes. True, you will have your redo log files for recovering the very latest transactions. But consider transactions that occurred since your last backup—which might have been hours ago—that are no longer on the redo log files because the redo log files now contain more recent transactions. Without archive log files, these older transactions are gone forever, rendering the more recent ones useless. Therefore, if you are not archiving your redo log files and a media failure occurs, you cannot recover all your data. The best you can do is to restore from backup, bringing your database up to the state it was in when the backup began.

The one exception to the rule that you cannot achieve full recovery from media failure without archive log files is if the failure occurs very shortly after you made the backup. In this case, your online redo log files will contain all the transactions made after the backup, so you will be able to restore your backed up data and recover your more recent data. But certainly you cannot count on this situation: the only way to be certain that you will be able to recover after a media failure is to enable archiving.

Enabling Archiving

To enable archiving for a database if archiving is not already enabled, use the ALTER DATABASE command with the ARCHIVELOG option. To make archiving automatic—that is, without further work by you—set the LOG_ARCHIVE_START initialization parameter to TRUE.

To tell the Server which file to archive to, set another initialization parameter, LOG_ARCHIVE_DEST, to the file specification. On some operating systems, you can specify a file that is on a tape. This is useful because tape is not only inexpensive, but portable: you can easily store tapes containing your archive in a separate location, such as a tape library or offsite storage.

If your operating system does not allow you to specify a tape drive destination, ensure fault tolerance by specifying a file on a device other than the one containing data files, redo log files, or the control file.

How Archiving Works

Automatic archiving works through the Archiver process (ARCH). Archiving begins just after a log switch occurs, and continues until ARCH has completely copied the redo log file. If you have only two online redo log files or log groups, then even if LGWR has filled the second redo log file, it cannot switch back to the first redo log file until ARCH has finished archiving the first file. If you have more than two redo log files, though, it's unlikely that LGWR will have to wait for ARCH to finish.

Another Reason to Use ARCHIVELOG Mode

There is another advantage to using the ARCHIVELOG option. In addition to protecting your database against media failure, this option allows you to make online database backups. As discussed earlier, the only way to recreate a consistent database after restoring with an online backup is to have created the backup while archiving is enabled. If NOARCHIVELOG mode is the current choice, you can only make consistent backups by shutting down the instance and closing the database.

READ-ONLY TABLESPACES

Version 7.1 of the Oracle Server introduces a feature that eliminates the need for backing up parts of a database that don't change: read-only tablespaces.

ADVANTAGE OF READ-ONLY TABLESPACES

A *read-only tablespace* is one to which no user can write. Because nobody can write to it, its data remains static. Therefore, once the data files in such a tablespace are backed up, they never need to be backed up again, so long as the tablespace remains read-only.

Designating a tablespace as read-only has several benefits. Backing up a large data file is time-consuming, and if the data does not change, then such backup is a waste of time. By the same token, a read-only tablespace does not have to be recovered—only restored from backup—in the case of a media failure. Furthermore, because the data does not change, you can store a read-only tablespace on a read-only medium such as CD-ROM, saving disk space for data that does change.

CANDIDATES FOR READ-ONLY TABLESPACES

What kind of data can reside in a read-only tablespace? Basically, any kind of data that doesn't change but that needs to be available for retrieval is a good candidate. (If the data does not need to be available for retrieval, then the tablespace can be simply taken offline.) Examples of candidates for read-only tablespaces include text of the tax law for the current year or information about all the films in a classic-film archive.

MAKING A TABLESPACE READ-ONLY

By default, a tablespace is in read-write mode; that is, database users can read from data files in it and write to these data files. To change a tablespace to read-only, use the ALTER TABLESPACE command with the READ ONLY option. For example, to make the OLD_DATA tablespace read-only, use the following command:

```
SQLDBA> ALTER TABLESPACE old_data
        READ ONLY;
```

DISTRIBUTED PROCESSING

CHAPTER OVERVIEW

In its broadest sense, distributed processing means performing a set of tasks across more than one processor. The Oracle7 Server is built with distributed processing in mind because it only deals with the database-management part of a database system, letting other programs handle the front-end work.

In this chapter, we examine distributed processing in a narrower sense: dividing a database among two or more networked computers. To use the features described in this chapter, you need the Oracle7 Server with the Distributed Option.

WHY USE DISTRIBUTED DATABASES?

The idea behind distributed databases is to allow users in one place to access data stored in another place. Suppose you are a manager in a large consulting company. You are located in San Francisco, but the company has offices and employees all over the world. Each branch keeps training records of its employees in a TRAINING database. When a consulting project comes to you from a local customer, you need to find employees who have the skills to complete the assignment. You query your database, but you find that none of the consultants in San Francisco has all the skills that the client needs. So, in order to staff the project properly, you must look to other branch offices.

This scenario is more common than you might think. In fact, to take advantage of distributed databases, the data does not have to be around the world or across the country. A local library or video-rental store has the same data-processing need when a patron requests an item that's checked out but that might be available in another nearby branch.

Oracle7 allows users to perform the same tasks with a remote database that they can with a local one, assuming they have the proper privileges. Users can not only select data from a remote database, but they can update and insert as well.

SQL*NET

For a client to communicate with a remote server (a server on another machine), the client and server must generally be connected through physical cable and must be using the same networking protocol, such as TCP/IP. The protocol is the set of standards dictating how data should be transmitted between client and server. When the data to be transmitted consists of SQL code or the results of SQL queries, then both client and server need an additional networking layer: an Oracle product called SQL*Net.

The main purpose behind SQL*Net is to make applications network-independent. The work that SQL*Net does—packaging the SQL code and data for transmission via the underlying network communications software—would have to be done by the client application if SQL*Net were not present. This would put too great a burden on the application developer, particularly when the application moves from one type of network to another. For example, if the application had been developed on a TCP/IP network but needed to be deployed in a DECnet environment, the programmer would have to recode all the parts of the application that dealt with TCP/IP to work with DECnet.

SQL*Net makes this extra work unnecessary, and the programmer can focus on developing an easy-to-use, robust application.

GLOBAL NAMES, DATABASE LINKS, AND SYNONYMS

When data is distributed among several computers, there needs to be a way to identify database objects uniquely and to describe their locations, so that users can access objects on remote machines. Global names and database links provide the means, and synonyms hide the complexity of the names.

GLOBAL NAMES

A database's unique identifier in a distributed system is its *global name*. Unlike a local name, which merely identifies a database on a single machine, the global name is unique among all databases. For a global name to be unique, it must identify both the local name of the database and the location of the database on the network.

Identifying the database is easy: it is the name you gave when you created the database. It is also the value of the DB_NAME parameter in the initialization file.

Identifying the location on the network is a little more complicated because it means specifying the network domain, which might require several levels for uniqueness. For example, it is not enough to refer to the domain VIDEOSPLUS if the company contains more than one division with a particular database name. (Figure 12.1)

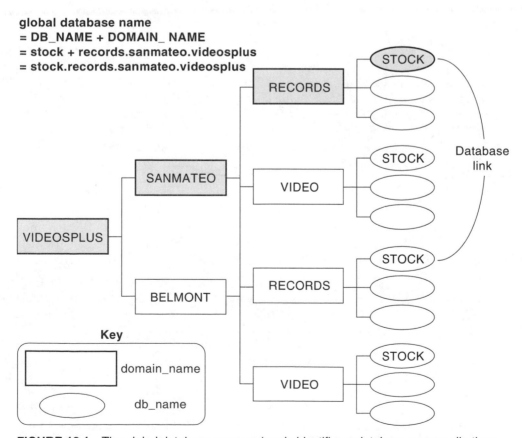

global database name
= DB_NAME + DOMAIN_ NAME
= stock + records.sanmateo.videosplus
= stock.records.sanmateo.videosplus

FIGURE 12.1 The global database name uniquely identifies a database among all others.

GLOBAL_NAMES Initialization Parameter

If you use distributed databases, Oracle Corporation recommends that you set the GLOBAL_NAMES initialization parameter to TRUE. Setting it to TRUE tells the Server to check whether a database link has the same name as the global name of the database it connects to; if it doesn't have the same name, the link does not work.

To specify the location, use the DB_DOMAIN parameter in the initialization file.

The combination of DB_NAME and DB_DOMAIN makes up the global database name. For example, if DB_NAME is STOCK and the database belongs to the RECORDS.SANMATEO.VIDEOSPLUS domain, then the global database name is STOCK.RECORDS.SANMATEO.VIDEOSPLUS.

DATABASE LINKS

A *database link* is the logical pathname of a remote database. Before a user can access a remote database, a database link must exist for the remote database in the local database, the one to which the user is connected. For example, if a user is connected to STOCK.RECORDS.SANMATEO.VIDEOSPLUS and wants to connect to STOCK.RECORDS.BELMONT.VIDEOSPLUS, then the database link for RECORDS.BELMONT.VIDEOSPLUS must exist in the RECORDS.SANMATEO.-VIDEOSPLUS database.

Creating a Database Link

As you can see from this example, the database link has the same name as the global database name (though if GLOBAL_NAMES is set to FALSE, the names do not have to be the same). To create a database link, just use the global database name in the CREATE DATABASE LINK command.

For example, in order to create a database link to STOCK.RECORDS.-BELMONT.VIDEOSPLUS that is available to all users of the database STOCK.RECORDS.SANMATEO.VIDEOSPLUS, simply issue the following command:

```
SQL> CREATE PUBLIC DATABASE LINK
  2  stock.records.belmont.videosplus;
```

This example assumes that a SQL*Net connect string has been specified in another public database link. A discussion of SQL*Net connect strings is beyond the scope of this book.

Once the database link is created, you can issue SQL statements that refer to objects in the remote database. To refer to a remote object, you must specify not only the object name, but also the schema to which the object belongs and the database link.

For example, if you are referring to the table NEW_RELS that is part of the database to which you are currently connected, the following statement would be valid:

```
SQL> SELECT title, artist
  2  FROM new_rels;
```

If, however, NEW_RELS is on a remote database, you must issue the following query:

```
SQL> SELECT title, artist
  2  FROM zemeckis.new_rels@stock.records.belmont.videosplus;
```

From this discussion, it might seem that anybody who knows about a public database link can get data from a remote database, and that database links therefore pose a security threat. In reality, though, using a database link is not enough to establish a connection to a remote Server. Every user who needs to use a remote database must have the CREATE SESSION privilege on the remote database, along with all other privileges required to perform various tasks. For example, if a local user needs to be able to update the remote table NEW_RELS, then the user needs the UPDATE object privilege on the remote database containing NEW_RELS.

Viewing Available Database Links

Because information about database links is stored in the data dictionary of the local database, users can find out which databases are available to them by querying data dictionary views. Entering the following command tells you which database links you can use:

```
SQL> SELECT db_link
  2  FROM all_db_links;
```

This command only works if GLOBAL_NAMES is set to TRUE. Ordinarily, though, users will not have to use this command because the database administrator and application developer will have provided all the database links that users will need to do their work. As a DBA, however, you might want to see all the database links in the database that's currently open, along with the username of the owner of the link. To do so, you would enter the following command:

```
SQLDBA> SELECT db_link, owner
           FROM dba_db_links;
```

SYNONYMS

Rather than use the entire database link name to refer to a remote database, you can create a synonym defined in terms of the database link name, and then use the synonym in subsequent SQL statements.

For example, you can issue the following command to define the synonym BELSTOCK:

```
SQL> CREATE SYNONYM belstock
  2  FOR stock.records.belmont.videosplus;
```

Now, the query mentioned earlier can be issued using the following statement:

```
SQL> SELECT title, artist
  2  FROM zemeckis.new_rels@belstock;
```

A synonym can be used for any schema object, not just database links. But it is particularly suitable for database links because those names can get quite long.

TWO-PHASE COMMIT: DATA CONSISTENCY IN A DISTRIBUTED DATABASE

SOME DEFINITIONS

So far, we've been talking about *remote queries* and *remote updates*. Such statements get data or modify data on a single remote machine. But in many cases, you may want to simultaneously get data from two or more databases located on different machines. For example, our record-store clerk might want to find all the branches that carry a particular title, instead of searching through each branch's database one by one. A statement that would perform such a query is called a *distributed query*. Similarly, a statement that updates more than one database is called a *distributed update*.

A series of remote queries or updates makes up a *remote transaction*. A transaction that contains one or more distributed queries or updates is called a *distributed transaction*.

POTENTIAL PROBLEMS

You will recall from our discussion of data consistency that a transaction consists of the related statements between COMMIT or ROLLBACK statements. You will also recall that the Oracle Server keeps data consistent from the beginning of a transaction to the end: if a failure occurs in the middle of a transaction, all non-committed statements will be rolled back.

But now consider the difficulty in doing this when several databases on different nodes are involved in a distributed transaction. To appreciate the importance of the problem, consider the following situation.

A bank customer is transferring $1000 from her savings account to her checking account. While this is one transaction, it actually involves two steps:

Step One: Subtract $1000 from Savings

Step Two: Add $1000 to Checking

Assume that her bank keeps all savings-account data on one computer and all checking-account data on another. Each computer's database is controlled by its own copy of the Oracle Server, and the bank teller uses a smaller computer running a graphical application to handle such banking transactions. The following illustration shows the configuration. (Figure 12.2)

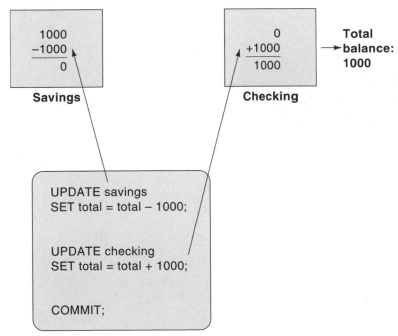

FIGURE 12.2 Successful distributed transaction.

While the application has a simple user interface, so that the teller can simply click a TRANSFER button, the underlying code includes both these distributed updates. By clicking TRANSFER, specifying the "FROM" account and "TO" account, and entering the dollar amount, the teller gives the application all the inputs it needs to tell the Servers what to do. If everything is working properly, the total account balance (savings plus checking) remains the same.

But what happens if a network failure occurs over the part of the network connecting the client to the CHECKING database? Such a failure could prevent the checking account from being credited, while the savings account will have been debited, since it is on a computer unaffected by the network failure. The result is that the total balance in savings and checking is $1000 less than when the transaction began. Clearly, this situation is unacceptable. Even the bank would probably agree! (Figure 12.3)

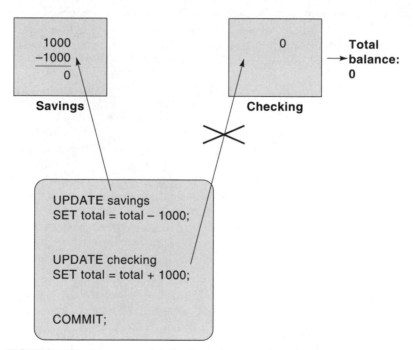

FIGURE 12.3   Unsuccessful distributed transaction, due to network failure.

That undesirable situation can only happen if one Server has received a COMMIT while the other one has not. What needs to happen instead is for all statements to roll back, and that is exactly what the Oracle Server guarantees will happen. It does so through a mechanism called the *two-phase commit*. With the two-phase commit, all statements in a distributed transaction must commit for the transaction to commit; otherwise, the entire transaction rolls back.

HOW A TWO-PHASE COMMIT WORKS

Unlike a regular commit, which consists entirely of the commit phase, a two-phase commit starts with a prepare phase. During this phase, the node issuing the COMMIT (called the *initiating node* or the *global coordinator*) asks other nodes involved in the transaction to prepare to commit or roll back the transaction. If a participating node agrees to prepare, its copy of the Oracle Server writes the transaction's redo entries to its redo log files, but it does so only for those redo entries for the statements modifying data on that site. That way, if a failure occurs affecting that node, the node's Server can still commit the transaction, just as other nodes' Servers are committing their portion of it.

After writing the redo information to file, the prepared node tells the global coordinator that it has prepared. When the global coordinator has received a "prepared" message from each of the participating nodes, the commit phase begins and the transaction ends just as a non-distributed transaction would. (Figure 12.4)

Instead of "prepared," a participating node can send the global coordinator a "read-only" response—that is, that the transaction has not changed any data in the node. Since unchanged data does not have to be committed or rolled back, the "read-only" response is acceptable for the commit phase to begin.

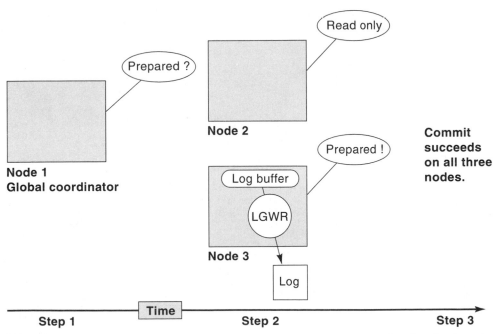

FIGURE 12.4 Two-phase commit ending in a commit on all nodes, leaving the distributed database in a consistent state.

If, however, a node cannot prepare to participate in a coordinated commit, the transaction never enters the commit phase. Instead, the problem node rolls back its part of the transaction and sends an "abort" message to the global coordinator, thus telling it that other nodes should roll back also. (

The initiating node frequently, but not always, serves as the *commit point site*. The commit point site is the first node to commit its part of the transaction, as directed by the global coordinator. The commit point site stores the most important data and never enters the prepare phase because the end of the prepare phase, by definition, signals that the transaction thus far is "in doubt" in that it has not yet been committed.

If the commit point site does commit successfully, then all nodes will eventually have to commit, even if a failure occurs. To tell other nodes that it has committed, the commit point site tells the global coordinator, which tells the other nodes to commit.

Once all sites are committed, the two-phase commit is complete and the data on all nodes is consistent.

If the commit point site does not commit (for example, if a failure occurs that prevents it from doing so), then the entire transaction is rolled back on all nodes. (Figure 12.5)

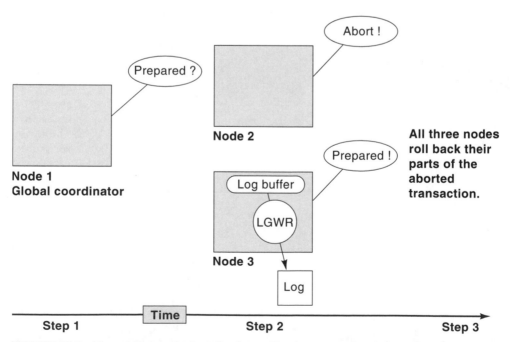

FIGURE 12.5 Two-phase commit ending in a rollback on all nodes, leaving the distributed database in a consistent state.

REPLICATION

Distributed processing can have drawbacks. Network traffic can cause delays, while network failures can prevent clients from using a remote database altogether. To avoid these problems, the Oracle Server includes a feature, Replication, that allows users to access a local copy of data that resides on another machine. Through replication, DBAs can create an environment where users can continue accessing remote data even when the remote database is down or otherwise inaccessible.

READ-ONLY SNAPSHOTS

If your users' only reason for accessing a remote database is to query information, and if the information changes infrequently or if it's not critical that users see the very latest data, it may be a good idea to create a *read-only snapshot* of the data you need.

What Is a Snapshot?

As its name suggests, a snapshot is a copy of some data at a particular moment. This copy does not get updated whenever its master table gets updated; instead, the Server updates the snapshots only after specified intervals. This deferred update behavior is sometimes called *asynchronous replication*.

A *complex* read-only snapshot can be based on data that is on one or more tables, views, or other snapshots, and it can be defined in terms of parts of these master objects—such as three columns of a master table or only certain rows of the master table.

A *simple* read-only snapshot, in contrast, is based on data that is on a single master table. For example, to create a snapshot based on the NEW_RELS table of STOCK.RECORDS.SANMATEO.VIDEOSPLUS, you might issue the following command:

```
SQL> CREATE SNAPSHOT new_rels_snap
  2    REFRESH COMPLETE
  3    START WITH sysdate
  4    NEXT sysdate + 1
  5    AS SELECT * FROM new_rels@stock.records.sanmateo.videosplus;
```

Notice that line 5 of the CREATE SNAPSHOT command above contains the actual query on which the snapshot is based. In this example, the snapshot is based on a simple remote query which gets data from just one table.

Refreshing a Snapshot

When you create a snapshot, you specify how frequently it should be refreshed. Recall that in SQL date arithmetic, time is measured in days. In the example above, NEW_RELS_SNAP gets refreshed daily, as indicated by line 4 of the SQL statement that creates the snapshot. For other snapshots, you might choose a less frequent refresh interval. For example, if you are administering a database for a national grocery-store chain, where headquarters change prices weekly, you would set the refresh interval to seven days. Each node on which you have created the snapshot, then, would receive an updated price list once each week.

Using SQL's date arithmetic, you can specify a refresh interval of hours or minutes by defining it as a fraction of a day. For example, to specify an hourly refresh, use the following line in your CREATE SNAPSHOT statement:

```
NEXT sysdate + 1/24
```

Similarly, to specify a refresh every minute, use the following line in your CREATE SNAPSHOT statement:

```
NEXT sysdate + 1/1440
```

UPDATABLE SNAPSHOTS

Suppose you want the ability to make changes to data on a remote table, as well as enjoy the advantages of snapshots. You can use a new, optional feature of Version 7.1, the Symmetric Replication Facility, which provides the ability to create an *updatable snapshot*.

What Is an Updatable Snapshot?

In many ways, an updatable snapshot is similar to a read-only snapshot: both are based on remote queries and both get refreshed at regular intervals. The main difference is that you can make changes to an updatable snapshot, changes that ultimately get propagated back to the master table. Another difference is that an updatable snapshot must be simple. It can only be defined in terms of one remote master table, and must query the entire table instead of only certain columns.

For example, the following command creates an updatable snapshot on the NEW_RELS table:

```
SQL> CREATE SNAPSHOT new_rels_update_snap FOR UPDATE
  2    REFRESH COMPLETE
  3    START WITH sysdate
  4    NEXT sysdate + 1
  5    AS SELECT * FROM new_rels@stock.records.sanmateo.videosplus;
```

The only difference between this command and the one for creating a read-only snapshot is the FOR UPDATE clause in line 1. As you might imagine, though, updatable snapshots pose some technical challenges that read-only snapshots do not. Therefore, issuing this command is not enough to create a working updatable snapshot. At each site, you must also call several packaged procedures that are shipped with the Symmetric Replication Facility, in order to set up the replication environment for that site.

Propagating Snapshot Changes to the Master Table

Whenever you make a change to an updatable snapshot, an entry of the change gets stored in the site's *deferred transaction table*. When you call a procedure to apply the changes made to the snapshot back to the master table, the snapshot site uses the deferred transaction table to send a list of its changes (along with the old values) to the master site. To prevent unintentional overwrites of data in the master table, the Symmetric Replication Facility looks for conflicting data by comparing the old values sent from the snapshot site with the corresponding current values at the master site. If the values match, then the master table underwent no changes to the rows that changed in the snapshot. A difference between the values, on the other hand, indicates that the row in conflict was modified on the master table, and that simply applying the snapshot's changes would overwrite the master's changes.

Therefore, the Server uses one or more conflict-resolution routines (chosen when you set up the snapshot site's replication environment) to determine what value to apply to the master table. For example, one resolution might be to compare the new snapshot value with the current master table value and apply the value with the more recent timestamp, regardless of whether this value is from the master site or the snapshot site. Another resolution might be to apply both, additively. Yet another resolution might be to apply the average of the values. In any case, once the Symmetric Replication Facility determines how to resolve the conflict, it applies the appropriate value to the master table. Unresolved conflicts get stored in an error table, giving the DBAs the freedom to resolve the conflicts any way they choose.

For rows where there is no conflict, the facility simply applies the new values sent from the snapshot site.

As a result of this process, the master table contains changes made to the updatable snapshot, as well as changes made directly to the master.

Refreshing Updatable Snapshots

You don't have to refresh updatable snapshots as frequently as you propagate snapshot changes to the master. For example, you might choose a refresh interval of one day while sending updates to the master table every five minutes.

No matter what your refresh interval, the Symmetric Replication Facility makes sure that changes made to the updatable snapshots are not lost during refresh. You might expect conflict-resolution routines to solve this problem, just as they do when snapshots propagate their changes to the master table. But this is not the method used by the Symmetric Replication Facility. Instead, the facility concentrates all conflict resolution at the master site, just before the refresh happens. Changes logged in the deferred transaction queue get sent to the master and are applied as described in the previous section. Then, the refresh occurs; as a result, the master table and the snapshot are once again synchronized.

PARALLEL PROCESSING

CHAPTER OVERVIEW

Generally speaking, database growth degrades performance. It takes the Server longer to process requests if there are more users or if users are requesting larger amounts of data. One way to maintain or improve performance is to add more CPUs by clustering several computers into a loosely coupled system. Another is to use multiprocessing computers. This chapter describes how the Oracle Server can take advantage of such configurations.

PARALLEL SERVER

The Parallel Server Option is a special feature of the Oracle Server that allows two or more instances to access the same database. What does this really mean, and why is it special?

WHAT IS THE PARALLEL SERVER?

To understand the Parallel Server, it helps to recall how its counterpart, the Server running in exclusive mode, works. In an exclusive configuration, one instance mounts and opens a particular database. That instance's SGA contains all the memory buffers associated with that database, and applications accessing the data can only access it as fast as that one instance permits. True, by using database links applications can access data in a database to which they are not directly connected, but they can do so only by connecting to the instance that is directly connected to the remote database. In other words, even in a distributed configuration, only one instance can access a database at a time.

In a Parallel Server configuration, by contract, several instances access the same database in parallel. How does this work? It works partly through the use of the underlying hardware of a *loosely coupled* computer system. In a loosely coupled, or *clustered*, system, several processors on different nodes can work at the same time, and each node has its own memory. At the same time, though, all the nodes in the cluster share files on disks. The Oracle Parallel Server uses this system by mapping the SGA of each instance to a separate memory area and by running each instance's background processes on a separate processor. The database's data files, though, are shared by all the instances. Thus, in a Parallel Server configuration, several instances access the same database. (Figure 13.1)

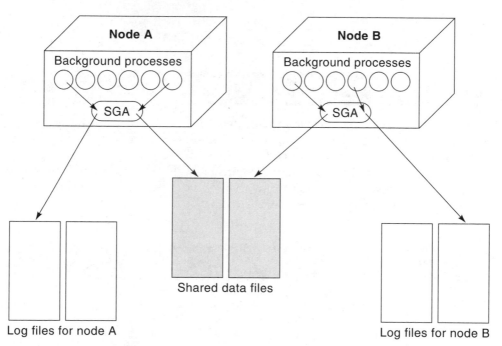

FIGURE 13.1 In a Parallel Server configuration, several instances in a loosely coupled system share one set of data files. Each instance has its own redo log files.

ADVANTAGES OF THE PARALLEL SERVER

For several reasons, using the Oracle Parallel Server is better than using the Oracle Server in exclusive mode.

Continuous Access

The obvious advantage of having several instances running is that if one fails, others are up and available for handling application requests. Since SQL statements refer to a database, not a particular instance, applications can continue accessing a database that is opened in parallel mode as if nothing happened, particularly if the Parallel Server is running in a cluster with automatic failover. Users can access the database 24 hours a day, seven days a week. Clearly, such high availability is impossible without the Parallel Server, no matter how quick recovery is.

Faster Processing

By splitting up the work of handling requests from applications among multiple processors, the Parallel Server improves performance.

Greater Flexibility

The Oracle Parallel Server gives DBAs more options in planning their databases. Whereas in the past they might have split up related data among different nodes to achieve faster processing, with data on each node managed by its own copy of the Oracle Server and possibly by its own DBA, DBAs who have the use of the Parallel Server can consolidate databases onto one loosely coupled system.

Also, with the Parallel Server, DBAs can more easily manage database growth. Instead of just adding disks to hold the extra data files of a larger database, DBAs can add cluster nodes to process the extra workload of larger databases and more users.

While each instance in a Parallel Server configuration accesses the same data files, each instance has its own redo log and control files. This ensures that in the case of a failure to one of the instances, only that instance's transactions get reapplied.

HOW THE PARALLEL SERVER WORKS

The Parallel Server is not simply the Oracle Server sitting on top of a loosely coupled system. It presents some special challenges.

Cache Coherency and Transaction Isolation

For the Parallel Server to work right, the data in all the SGAs must be consistent. This characteristic—copies of the most recent version of a data block in multiple SGAs being identical—is called *cache coherency*. Cache coherency prevents the lost-update problem discussed in Chapter 6. Furthermore, the Parallel Server— just like standard Oracle7—must prevent the possibility of dirty reads. In other words, the database system must ensure *transaction isolation*, so that changes made by an uncommitted transaction are not visible to other transactions (on the same node or another node) until the first transaction ends in a commit.

As discussed in earlier chapters, standard Oracle7 has performance features such as row-level locking, fast commits, and deferred writes. Since a major purpose of the Parallel Server is high performance, the Parallel Server maintains these features. At the same time, though, the Parallel Server must ensure transaction isolation and cache coherency. In other words, users on any two or more nodes should see the same data, and actions on one node should not overwrite changes on another node.

We have already seen how Oracle's lock manager ensures that one transaction does not overwrite the changes made by a concurrent transaction. But to coordinate activities among nodes, where data resides in several SGAs, an internode locking mechanism is necessary. Operating systems that work on loosely coupled systems have such a mechanism, usually called the Distributed Lock Manager (DLM). Oracle's Parallel Server uses the DLM of the underlying operating system to solve some internode data consistency problems.

Using the DLM presents some potential performance problems, however. If there is too much DLM activity, particularly excessive communication among the nodes, the cluster will not scale well: DLM operations could increase exponentially for every node that's added. Thus, potential performance gains achieved through adding nodes would be offset by the cost of too much DLM activity.

To prevent this performance problem, the Oracle Parallel Server minimizes the role of the DLM, while still maintaining data consistency. It does so by using the DLM only for cache coherency. Transaction isolation, in contrast, gets taken care of through the same mechanisms used by the Oracle Server running in exclusive mode.

An Example

A simple example illustrates the process. Assume four users, two on each node in a cluster: Anne and Alan are connected to an instance on node A; Betty and Bruce are connected to an instance on node B.

When Anne needs to update a row, she reads in the data block containing the row into the SGA of node A. Two events happen:

❏ The Oracle Server locks the row to be modified, preventing Alan from updating it. Because this is a row-level lock, Alan can modify other rows in the block. (This is standard Oracle7 behavior.)

❏ The DLM acquires an exclusive lock on the block, preventing users on node B from modifying the block. (This is special Parallel Server behavior.)

When Anne commits her transaction, several events happen:

❏ LGWR writes an entry in a redo log file. (This is the "fast commit" behavior of standard Oracle7.)

❏ The Server releases the row lock. (This, too, is standard behavior.)

❏ The DLM keeps its exclusive lock on the block. (This behavior is special to the Parallel Server.) Why the DLM keeps the lock becomes clear when you consider what might happen next.

Betty tries to update a row in the same block; she cannot do so immediately because node A holds an exclusive DLM lock on the block. If she were allowed to read the block from disk into node B's SGA and then modify it, the block would hold different values in the two SGAs. This would be a cache coherency problem, causing destructive interference when the two different copies of the block get written to disk. But Betty does need to update the block. Here's how the Parallel Server handles the situation:

❏ The DLM tells node A that it needs to release the lock.

❏ Since releasing the lock while keeping the modified block in node A's SGA jeopardizes cache coherency, a lock process (LCK0, for example) tells DBWR to write the modified block to a data file. That way, the block that Betty reads into node B's SGA will contain all of Anne's changes. As you can see, the write by DBWR is a deferred one—just as in exclusive mode—because it did not occur as soon as Anne's transaction ended.

In this example, you can see that only the work necessary to achieve cache coherency is done by the DLM. To achieve transaction isolation with high concurrency, the Parallel Server uses Oracle's row-level locking mechanism and fast commits.

What may not be clear from this example, because Anne and Betty's transactions contend for the same data block, is that the DLM only communicates between instances when one instance needs to access a block held in the SGA of another instance. If multiple instances are accessing different blocks from the same database, they can do so without any internode communication.

As a result of the reduced scope of DLM activity and of the division of labor between the DLM and the Oracle lock manager, the DLM does not counteract the performance gains of multiple processors. In fact, the Parallel Server achieves near-linear scaling: throughput (as measured by transactions per second) increases in almost direct proportion to the number of nodes in the cluster. (Figure 13.2)

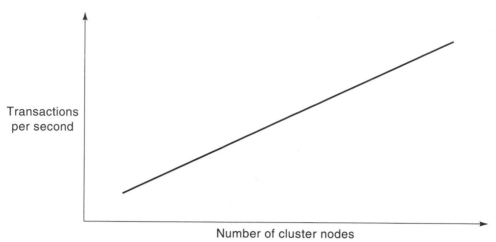

FIGURE 13.2 The Parallel Server scales linearly as nodes are added to the cluster on which it runs.

PARALLEL QUERIES

Version 7.1 of the Oracle Server introduces a feature that greatly speeds up the processing of queries on some computers. The feature, the Parallel Query Option, allows the Oracle Server to divide the work of executing a single query among several processors. The Parallel Query Option also enables faster indexing and data loading, but this chapter deals only with parallel queries.

USES

The best use of parallel queries is on large databases that are used for decision support. Such applications are characterized by long-running queries, which read data from large portions of a database. For example, a program that generates several weekly reports showing the usage of all parts in inventory ordered by type could run more quickly through the use of the parallel query option.

Contrast this application to a typical OLTP (online transaction-processing) application, such as one used by bank tellers to update individual accounts and give account information. This application is characterized by frequent database access, a combination of short reads and writes, and many users accessing the database at the same time. It would not be a good candidate for the Parallel Query Option; instead, it might benefit from the multithreaded server.

HOW PARALLEL QUERYING WORKS

When a user issues a query, a single server process, called the *query coordinator*, determines which operations of the execution plan can be broken up and performed simultaneously by different processors; the query coordinator then assigns these operations to several other processes, called *query servers*. (In contrast, if you are not using the Parallel Query Option, only one server process works on behalf of each query.) Each of the query servers performs its assigned suboperation and returns the result to the query coordinator, which assembles the results and returns them to the user. (Figure 13.3)

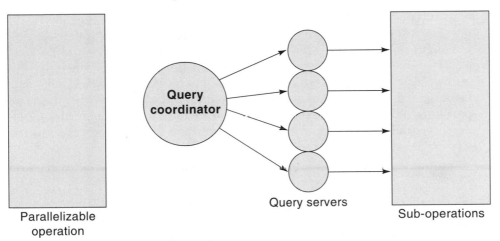

Parallelizable operation
Query servers
Sub-operations

FIGURE 13.3 The query coordinator divides up the work of an operation among several query servers.

Operations That Can Be Parallelized

A query can be parallelized only if its execution plan includes a full table scan. If another access method is available (such as through a range search or a hash cluster key), and the optimizer chooses this other method over a full table scan, then the Server will execute the query using just one processor: it will not parallelize the query.

If, however, the optimizer chooses an execution plan that uses a full table scan, and if several processors are available, then the Server will parallelize the query, including other operations in the query that can be parallelized. Besides a full table scan, Version 7.1 of the Oracle Server can parallelize all types of sort operations and various join operations.

An Example

For example, consider the following query:

```
SQL> SELECT student_id, last_name, first_name
  2  FROM students
  3  ORDER BY student_id, last_name;
```

Assume the optimizer chooses an execution plan in which the access method is a full table scan. The optimizer then creates an execution plan:

1. scan STUDENTS

2. sort the rows by STUDENT_ID

The query coordinator first divides the table into groups of contiguous blocks, based on the number of query servers for this query. For example, if five query servers will be working on each operation in this query, the query coordinator might delineate five large groups, five smaller groups, five groups that are smaller than that, and five groups that are smaller than any of the others. Each query server starts by scanning a large group of blocks. When it's done scanning the large partition, it moves on to a smaller one, and so on until the very smallest partitions have been scanned. The idea is for all query servers to finish at the same time, regardless of their individual processing rates. As query servers finish, they return their results to the query coordinator.

Meanwhile, the first sort operation can begin. The partitioning requirement for a sort operation is different from the one for a table scan, because with a sort, the order of the result set is significant. Therefore, the query coordinator assigns each query server approximately the same number of rows based on the sort key. For example, if the values of STUDENT_ID range from 100001 to 600000, then the first query server would be assigned values 100001 through 200000; the second query server would be responsible for 200001 through 300000, and so on. As the results of the table scan operation come in from the first set of query servers, those query servers pass to each new query server those rows that are in its sort key range. Thus, a total of ten query servers are working on this query so far, though only five are working on any one operation.

When this second set of query servers is done, each one will have returned to the query coordinator a set of rows sorted by STUDENT_ID. The query coordinator puts these five sets in order and returns the result to the user.

HARDWARE AND DISK REQUIREMENTS

To make the Parallel Query Option work, you must use the right type of computer system with data distributed across multiple disks.

Multiprocessor Requirement

We have said that the Parallel Server Option requires a loosely coupled computer system, so that several instances can run in parallel, each using its own private memory but all sharing the same data files. Since a massively parallel processing computer is also a loosely coupled system, it too can be used for running the Parallel Server.

The Parallel Query Option, in contrast, does not require multiple instances (and hence a private memory region for each processor). Therefore, you can use the Parallel Query Option on any multiprocessor computer, including a single-node symmetric multiprocessor. In such a system, also called a *tightly coupled system*, multiple processors share not only disk resources but memory, as well.

Disk Requirements

Although the Parallel Query Option is flexible about the type of multiprocessing computer you use, it works well only if data is stored in a certain way.

When all the data to be scanned is on one disk, only one scan operation can occur at a time. The disk prevents any processor from performing its scan while another processor is in the middle of a scan. The situation is like having ten bakers using one small oven: since the oven can only hold one cake at a time, nine bakers are always sitting idle, so it takes almost as long for ten bakers to bake ten cakes as it would for one baker to bake them. Even though the workload may have been well parallelized, the work itself must proceed serially, undermining the whole point of multiple processors.

Therefore, to take advantage of the Parallel Query Option, table data should be distributed, or *striped*, across several disks. Ideally, you should use your operating system to implement file striping. If your operating system does not provide for automatic striping, however, you can achieve a similar—though less balanced—effect by manually striping data across files on different disks. You can do so when you specify data files in the CREATE TABLESPACE command and when you create the tables for that tablespace.

SPECIFYING HOW MANY PROCESSORS TO USE

You can tell the query coordinator how many query servers to use for a single operation. Doing so correctly is important for overall database performance: while using as many processors as are available to parallelize a single operation will, in fact, return quick results for the one query, it will hinder other statements that also depend on the computer's processors.

You can set the *degree of parallelism*, or the number of processors to be used for a single operation, in three places:

- ❏ the SQL statement itself, as a hint in a query
- ❏ the table definition, when creating or altering a table
- ❏   the initialization file

Hint in a Query

You can set the degree of parallelism in a hint that is part of your query. For example, the hint in the following query directs the Server to use four query processes for executing the query:

```
SQL> SELECT /*+ PARALLEL (students, 4) */ last_name, first_name
  2  FROM students
  3  ORDER BY last_name;
```

Using hints to specify the degree of parallelism does not make sense in ad hoc queries, but using them in an application is a relatively easy and effective way to tell the Server how many processes to use each time someone issues the query through the application.

Table Definition

You can also specify the degree of parallelism when creating a table. For example, if you want all queries on the STUDENTS table to use five query processes, use the following statement to create the table:

```
SQL> CREATE TABLE students
  2  (column definitions)
  3  PARALLEL 5;
```

After you create a table, you can change its degree of parallelism. For example, to change the degree of parallelism for STUDENTS to four, use the following command:

```
SQL> ALTER TABLE students
  2  PARALLEL 4;
```

Initialization Parameter File

If you don't specify a degree of parallelism in either the queried table or in the query itself, the Oracle Server bases the degree of parallelism on the values of two initialization parameters:

❏ PARALLEL_DEFAULT_MAX_SCANS specifies the maximum number of query servers to be used for any query.

❏ PARALLEL_DEFAULT_SCANSIZE sets the number of blocks each query server should scan. Thus, if a table has 500 blocks, and the value of PARALLEL_DEFAULT_SCANSIZE is 100, then five query servers are necessary to execute the query.

As you can see, the number of query servers specified by PARALLEL_DEFAULT_MAX_SCANS might be different from the number derived by dividing the table's blocks by PARALLEL_DEFAULT_SCANSIZE. To determine how many query servers to actually use, the Server uses the smaller of the two numbers.

For example, suppose you have set the parameters to the following values:

```
PARALLEL_DEFAULT_MAX_SCANS = 12
PARALLEL_DEFAULT_SCANSIZE = 500
```

You issue a query that needs to perform a full table scan on a table having 8,000 blocks. PARALLEL_DEFAULT_SCANSIZE would have the Server use 8,000/500 = 16 processors. Because 12, the value of PARALLEL_DEFAULT_MAX_SCANS, is less than 16, the Server would use 12 query servers.

Now consider a query on a smaller table, with the same initialization parameter values. This second table consists of 5,000 blocks. Thus, PARALLEL_-DEFAULT_SCANSIZE would have the Server use 5,000/500 = 10 query servers. Since 10 is less than 12, the Server would use only 10 query servers to scan this smaller table. But remember that if the table's definition or a hint in the query specifies a degree of parallelism, then the Server would use that degree of parallelism instead of the degree indicated by the initialization file.

Furthermore, no query can use more query servers than specified by PARALLEL_DEFAULT_MAX_SCANS. For example, if a query hint specifies the degree of parallelism to be 14 but PARALLEL_DEFAULT_MAX_SCANS = 12, the query would use only 12 query servers per operation.

INDEX

Numerics

64-bit architecture, and performance 108

A

access paths, rankings of 114
ALL_DB_LINKS data dictionary view 161
application-development tools
    automating the mechanics 8
    as creativity facilitators 8
applications
    custom 7
    ease of use of 4
    and enforcement of business rules 6
    and reduction of redundancy 5
ARCH 41
    and log sequence numbers 149
architecture, of an Oracle database 35
archived redo log files 154
ARCHIVELOG mode 147, 155
Archiver, *See* ARCH
archiving, enabling 154
archiving filled redo logs 154
asynchronous replication 167
auditing, for security 137–139
authentication
    choosing a method 122
    by the OS 122
    by the Server 122
availability, maximizing through Parallel Server 173

B

back ends 1–3
background processes 38–43
backing up a database 143–147
backup
    frequency of 147
    need for 143
    types of 143
backup and recovery 141–156
base tables, defined 22
binary data
    storing as LONG RAW 53
    storing as RAW 53
block information, data blocks 33
blocks, *See* data blocks
buffers, types of 46
built-in functions, in application-development tools 8
business rules, enforcing through applications 6

C

cache coherency 173
cache hit, defined 109